IMAGES OF WAR

BELSEN AND ITS LIBERATION

RARE PHOTOGRAPHS FROM WARTIME ARCHIVES

Ian Baxter

Pen & Sword
MILITARY

First published in Great Britain in 2014 by
PEN & SWORD MILITARY
An imprint of
Pen & Sword Books Ltd
47 Church Street
Barnsley
South Yorkshire
S70 2AS

ISBN 978-1-78159-331-8

Typeset by Concept, Huddersfield, West Yorkshire HD4 5JL.
Printed and bound in Malta by Gutenberg Press Ltd.

Pen & Sword Books Ltd incorporates the imprints of Pen & Sword Archaeology, Atlas, Aviation, Battleground, Discovery, Family History, History, Maritime, Military, Naval, Politics, Railways, Select, Social History, Transport, True Crime, and Claymore Press, Frontline Books, Leo Cooper, Praetorian Press, Remember When, Seaforth Publishing and Wharncliffe.

For a complete list of Pen & Sword titles please contact
PEN & SWORD BOOKS LIMITED
47 Church Street, Barnsley, South Yorkshire, S70 2AS, England
E-mail: enquiries@pen-and-sword.co.uk
Website: www.pen-and-sword.co.uk

Contents

About the Author

Ian Baxter is a military historian who specialises in German twentieth-century military history. He has written more than forty books including *Poland – The Eighteen Day Victory March*, *Panzers in North Africa*, *The Ardennes Offensive*, *The Western Campaign*, *The 12th SS Panzer-Division Hitlerjugend*, *The Waffen-SS on the Western Front*, *The Waffen-SS on the Eastern Front*, *The Red Army at Stalingrad*, *Elite German Forces of World War II*, *Armoured Warfare*, *German Tanks of War*, *Blitzkrieg*, *Panzer-Divisions at War*, *Hitler's Panzers*, *German Armoured Vehicles of World War Two*, *Last Two Years of the Waffen-SS at War*, *German Soldier Uniforms and Insignia*, *German Guns of the Third Reich*, *Defeat to Retreat: The Last Years of the German Army at War 1943–1945*, *Operation Bagration – the destruction of Army Group Centre*, *German Guns of the Third Reich*, *Rommel and the Afrika Korps*, *U-Boat War*, and most recently *The Sixth Army, the Road to Stalingrad*, *German Mountain Troops*, and *Himmler's Nazi Concentration Camp Guards*. He has also written over 100 articles including 'Last Days of Hitler', 'Wolf's Lair', 'Story of the V1 and V2 Rocket Programme', 'Secret Aircraft of World War Two', 'Rommel At Tobruk', 'Hitler's War with his Generals', 'Secret British Plans to Assassinate Hitler', 'SS At Arnhem', 'Hitlerjugend', 'Battle Of Caen 1944', 'Gebirgsjäger at War', 'Panzer Crews', 'Hitlerjugend Guerrillas', 'Last Battles in the East', 'Battle of Berlin' and many more. He has also reviewed numerous military studies for publication, supplied thousands of photographs and important documents to various publishers and film Production Companys worldwide, and lectures to various schools, colleges and universities throughout the United Kingdom and Southern Ireland.

Photographic Credits

Many of the photographs in this volume showing the liberation of Belsen were obtained with the kind permission of the Imperial War Museum in London. The photographs were taken by the British Army Film and Photographic Unit and prove beyond any reasonable doubt the pain and horror that was inflicted on the inmates of the camp.

Other photographs in this book were collected over a period of years by the author showing SS guards, notably the infamous *'Totenkopf'* (Death's Head) while training or on duty. Imagery by the Germans relating to the operations of Belsen is almost non-existent and unpublished material very scarce. The author has striven throughout to show in photographic form, at least to some degree, the life of the SS soldier while operating inside and outside the concentration camp. To maintain a balance, photographs from the Imperial War Museum have been used showing extensively the liberation and what the British found upon entering the camp.

Introduction

Belsen and Its Liberation is an illustrated record of how the Nazi's ran this notorious concentration camp. Originally established as a prisoner of war camp, Jewish hostages were held there with the intention of exchanging them for German prisoners of war held overseas. However, by 1943 the SS took over the camp and decided to expand the camp to accommodate Jews from other concentration camps. What followed were scenes of absolute horror and barbarity on a grand scale, perpetrated by both male and female guards. Accompanied by rare and unpublished photos, this book presents a unique visual account of one of history's most infamous episodes. Some of the imagery in it will show the murderous activities of individual SS-men inside Belsen, and reveal another disturbing side to them relaxing in their barracks or visiting their families and loved ones. The book provides an absorbing insight into how the SS played a key part in murdering, torturing and starving to death the inmates. During the latter part of the war, as many as 500 a day were perishing from the long-term effects of starvation and disease. The reader will find a wealth of information on how the camp was run and on all aspects of life for the inmates.

With the war dramatically drawing to an end, the final episode of Belsen is witnessed by British soldiers of the Second Army, who were neither physically nor psychologically prepared for what they encountered when they arrived at the gates of the camp. Inside the camp they were greeted with some 10,000 unburied dead, in addition to the mass graves which already contained 40,000 more corpses.

This volume captures the story of those that ran Belsen, those that perished, and the troops that liberated the living from their hell.

Profile of a Concentration Camp Guard

The barbaric behavior of concentration camp guards has raised some serious questions regarding the human capacity for evil. But the perpetrators as a whole were not sadists lusting for power and blood, or brainwashed by propaganda, or simply following orders. They had given themselves a personal choice to be or not to be evil. Many chose to be ruthless and brutal, and actually promoted the use of violence and terror.

Many of the SS who were posted to camps such as Belsen spoke about their personal experiences as if it was 'normal', except that rations for SS members were particularly good. Nowhere do they present themselves as mindless automatons that would have followed any command given to them. Although they were massively influenced by the propaganda of the times, it is evident from extensive research that they nevertheless made a series of personal choices. They carried on working in the concentration camps not just because they were ordered to but because, having weighed the evidence put before them, they thought that treating the inmates inside the camps inhumanely and killing them, was right. They could have easily rejected the values of their community, resisted and got posted to the front, but there is no record of any member of the SS ever having done so on moral grounds.

The men and women who were posted to Belsen regarded it as a particularly good posting, and felt what they were doing there was right. Although they were taught blind and absolute obedience to all orders from their SS superiors, on a number of occasions they felt able to criticize the way the camp was being run. They knew that they never needed to fear terrible retribution if they criticized an order because, strange as it may seem, the Nazi leadership allowed functionaries lower down the chain of command openly to use their initiative and voice their views. Many of them, whatever they may have professed to their captors at the end of the war, actually believed wholeheartedly in the Nazi vision, and this meant that they felt free to question the details of its implementation. Many of the guards knew that they had embarked on something that human beings had never attempted before – the systematic extermination of thousands of men, women, and children in a matter of months. These men and women in the camps had created killing factories, whether they were extermination camps with gas chambers, or such as Belsen where inmates were tortured, shot, starved and left to die disease ridden. They were concerned not about the suffering of the inmates, but about problems of how the camp would run smoothly and efficiently.

Most of the guards considered that they lived a tolerable life. Outside the camp they felt almost insulated from the brutality and were able to avert from their eyes from anything that displeased them. As guards they lived in comfortable barracks with several of their comrades. For the officers, life was better still. Many stayed with their families in requisitioned houses nearby; they enjoyed a standard of living that far surpassed anything they could have achieved had they been attached to a fighting unit. Here in their homes these men with their wives and children, had created a settled environment and, for the most part, they had found a successful way of distancing themselves from life in the concentration camp. Their families were never given any hint of what murderous activities their husbands and fathers were under-taking inside the camps. Almost every concentration camp operative was determined from the onset to conceal as much of this gruesome knowledge as possible from the outside world. In their own minds it was not just their oath of loyalty they were protecting, but their own credentials as human beings.

Profile of a Woman Concentration Camp Guard

Of the 55,000 guards who served in Nazi concentration camps, about 3,700 were women. In 1942, the first female guards arrived at Auschwitz and Majdanek from Ravensbrück. The year after, the Germans began conscripting women because of a guard shortage. Most women who were recruited to become overseers were middle to low class, from non-professional backgrounds, and had no work experience. As a group, the women guards were not highly regarded by their inmates, who were often educationally and culturally their superiors. Volunteers were mostly German women who were recruited by advertisements in newspapers asking women to show their love for the Reich by joining the *SS-Gefolge* (an *SS* cousin organization for women). A few entered the service this way, attracted to the promise of light physical work and good wages. But countless young women were recruited under stronger incentives from *SS* officials. They were told to choose between continuing their menial position indefinitely or joining the *SS*. The position of a women guard paid well, and in 1944 an unmarried women guard in her mid-twenties could make considerably more than she could as a textile worker. By 1943, the Reich Labour Ministry was empowered to conscript women between 17 and 45 years of age for labour service, and by the end of that year, most of the women reporting for concentration camp training were conscripts.

Ravensbrück served as the main training ground for some 3,700 female guards after 1938. Trainees spent anywhere from a week to six months at the camp, at first being given regulated instruction from the Head Overseer. The trainees were taught the standard regulations applicable to all concentration camps, 'how to detect sabotage and work slowdowns, how to prevent escapes, and how to punish prisoners within the parameters of camp regulations'. It was emphasized that female guards were to have no relationship of a personal nature with any of the prisoners. The guards were notoriously cruel. Yet not all women became accustomed to brutality. On the contrary, some were sympathetic to the needs of the prisoners. However, those that deviated from the standard mentality often faced despair and were severely punished as a result of their insubordination. In the eyes of their superiors their ultimate aim was to gradually accustom the recruits to the brutality of camp life, step by step. The nicknames given to some of the guards, such as the 'Beast of Auschwitz' and the 'Bitch of Buchenwald', are clear evidence of the success of this process. The simple-mindedness of some of the female guards made them more amenable to torment and kill the 'racially impure'. The internal structure of the individual concentration camps they would be sent to, all involved a method of mistreating the prisoners. The code of conduct for these female guards was based upon the SS demand for blind and absolute obedience to all orders from superior officers, and upon their insistence that each prisoner be regarded with fanatical hatred as an enemy of the state. By exhorting the women guards to constantly hate the prisoners, and simultaneously by buttressing this hatred with the legality of orders, they were enabled to mete out the harshest punishments to the prisoners.

Chapter One

POW Camp

Bergen-Belsen was a concentration camp constructed in northwestern Germany, southwest of the old town of Bergen in what was then the province of Hanover. It was originally built in 1935 as a *Wehrmacht* military complex training area and used to train armoured vehicle crews. While training was in progress the site was expanded and the workers who constructed the large complex were housed in camps near Fallingbostel. The site was not completed until 1938/39, and the workers' camp then fell into disuse.

It was not until September 1939, following the German invasion of Poland, that the Germans decided on using the old Fallingbostel camp huts as a Polish POW camp. These huts became known as Stalag XI-B and were expanded at a rapid rate during the Polish campaign. The expansion of the POW camp increased further when in May 1940 the Germans unleashed their forces against the Low Countries and France. The attack was once again swift and decisive, and soon French and Belgian POWs were pouring through the gates of Stalag XI-B.

By June 1940, following the defeat of France, some 80,000 prisoners were being held in the Bergen-Belsen camp. The following year in June 1941 the Germans attacked their old arch-enemy, the Soviet Union. The army at Belsen immediately set to work preparing the site for the large influx of Soviet prisoners that were soon to be expected, and turned it into an independent camp known as Stalag XI-C. One of three camps in the area, it was intended to hold some 20,000 Russian POWs. The other camps were at Oerbke Stalag XI-D and Wietzendorf Stalag X-D

Even the average *Wehrmacht* camp guard saw the Soviet Union as a land ripe for plunder. Many were firmly convinced that the Russians were an inferior race and had come to appreciate the Nazi views on Communism and Judaism. Within days of the German onslaught through the Russian heartlands there were rumours of ruthless actions against Russian Jews, Communist politicians and political commissars.

The first Soviet prisoners were transported to Belsen in late June 1941. Before they began their journey to the camp, those that were fit enough were led to one side, while those too weak to be moved were simply shot where they lay. The corpses were then dragged away by other prisoners into a pile for disposal. The journey to the camp was one of complete horror. When they arrived at Belsen, hundreds had already perished. Many of them had died of thirst or exhaustion on the journey. Several hundred of them were marched through the main gate and from the moment they arrived they were treated much worse than the Polish, Belgian, or French inmates. The Russians were especially hated at the camp. As soon as they entered the camp many of them were beaten and tortured, while many were left to starve to death. The POW camp itself was simply a square area of land where most of the Russians were huddled together in squalid looking huts made from wood. Food distribution was so irregular that most of the prisoners were constantly hungry and exhausted. For these hapless men, food was a matter of obsession. For weeks they had been reduced to scavenging. They were in terrible physical condition. Within days many of them were half dead, starving and full of lice. The prisoners lived like animals. They died of starvation, illness, injuries, and were subjected to more or less unrestrained killing. Their deaths brought more space for additional Russian prisoners and this in turn caused further starvation and death.

When winter arrived many of the Soviet prisoners were left exposed in freezing conditions. In late 1941 there was an outbreak of dysentery, and because they were unable to move due to the cramped conditions these frequently emaciated and broken men often soiled their own ragged clothes. Caked in mud and faeces the inmates just lay there in their own filth, too weak to maintain any shred of human dignity. As the first snow showers began to fall, the arctic temperatures dramatically increased the number of fatalities. By the end of March 1942, some 41,000 Soviet POWs had died in the three camps of starvation, exhaustion and disease.

However, 1942 had opened up with a series of major disappointments for the German Army in Russia. It had become clear that Operation Barbarossa, the code-name for the German invasion of the Soviet Union, had failed miserably and that Germany was compelled to mobilize all its resources to continue the war effort. With all men called up for service there were greater demands on German industry, especially in armaments. The armaments industry had become seriously under-manned and Russian POWs were diverted from POW camps to the armaments industry and work camps; pressure on the Belsen camp was relieved.

Throughout 1942 the Nazi regime continued with a policy of more or less unrestrained terror and murder. With this policy it effectively brought about the most radical ideas imaginable. The situation in the various detention centres and con-centration camps had become untenable due to the new policies of arresting and detaining enemies of the state. News had already circulated through SS channels that government officials were demanding immediate action in the expansion of the concentration camp system. The German authorities quickly pressed forward to establish various camps under the complete control of the SS. One such camp destined to be handed over to the SS Economic-Administration Main Office or *SS Wirtschafts-Verwaltungshauptamt* (WVHA) was Bergen Belsen.

The German invasion of Poland began in earnest on 1st September 1939. The attack was swift and victory by the Germans was secured in little over eighteen days. For the German soldier it was their first experience of the East, and the first time they had ever seen Eastern Jews, though they had seen these figures in many of the anti-Semitic drawings and posters plastered on notice boards, walls and lamp-posts throughout Germany.

In June 1941 the Germans invaded the Soviet Union. In German eyes, Russia was a land ripe for plunder. The Germans were firmly convinced that the Russians were an inferior race and had come to accept the Nazi theories of Communism and Judaism. Within days of the invasion there were ruthless actions against Russian Jews, Communist politicians and political commissars. In this photograph SS troops capture Soviet troops, of which many were transported to labour or concentration camps.

Wehrmacht troops round up Russian soldiers who have been captured. Many Soviet prisoners were transported to various labour camps throughout Germany and Poland. One such camp was a Stalag camp at Belsen. From the moment they arrived they were treated much worse than the Polish inmates. From 1941 to 1945 almost 20,000 Russian prisoners of war were killed or died of disease or malnutrition.

Russian POWs sit at the side of a road, awaiting a fate that they could only imagine. With so many Russian POWs falling into captivity, the SS had ordered that they were to be used as slave labour to build labour and concentration camps, mainly across Germany and Poland. Conditions inside the POW camp were reported to be appalling with many soldiers severely undernourished. At Stalag XI-C, X-D, XI-D at Belsen, conditions were horrific with many of the prisoners either being starved to death or dying of illness.

Two photographs showing Russian prisoners being rounded up by SS troops between 1941 and 1942. A number of these Russian POWs were sent to Belsen, which was initially an independent camp known as Stalag XI-C (311). This area held to up to 20,000 Soviet POWs and consisted of three camps in the area. The others were at Wietzendorf (Stalag X-D (310)) and Oerbke (Stalag XI-D (321)). By the end of March 1942, some 41,000 Soviet POWs had died in these three camps from starvation and disease.

A German MG34 machine gun crew march through a village towards the battlefront, being watched by local peasants moving the other way. For the average German soldier systematic murder of the local population and anti-Semitism were not at the forefront of his mind. However, he knew that the Soviet Union was a land ripe for plunder. Both Jews and Russian POWs were to be rounded up and sent to the rear for processing. However, many were not processed and were either murdered on the spot, or sent directly to Germany or Poland to be used in slave labour camps.

An *SS* commanding officer lectures his men on the march through Russia. An order from *SS Reichsführer* Heinrich Himmler had instructed that captured Russian soldiers were not to be disposed of immediately, but used as slave labour. Many of the POWs who were captured marched for days to the camps. The journey to Stalag Belsen camp was a journey of complete horror. By the time they arrived at the town of Belsen, hundreds had already perished.

SS motorcyclists near the town of Bergen-Belsen in 1941. It would not be until 1943 that the *SS* Economic-Administration Main Office (*SS Wirtschafts-Verwaltungshauptamt*, WVHA) would take over control of the Belsen camp. However, prior to this time *SS* troops assigned to guard duties were regularly seen accompanying POWs to the Stalag camps.

Russian locals are rounded up by the *Wehrmacht* suspected of being part of a resistance group. It is probable that these men were not taken to camps within Poland or Germany and used for slave labour, but executed on the spot for their alleged actions.

Across Eastern Europe the process of moving millions of Jews from the ghettos to labour and concentration camps was in full swing by the winter of 1942. Here in these four photographs Jews are being moved by train from unknown ghettos to destinations that can only be imagined. For many of the Jews who disembarked from the crammed cattle cars, the railway stops were often very much like any other provincial railway station they had been to. But these were far removed from anything they had ever endured. Under strict supervision of SS guards, *Kapos*, and local police they were routed through the local towns directly to the main labour or concentrations camps. Often, once they arrived at the camps there was hardly any water or washing facilities, and the weak and starving prisoners were living in utter filth and degradation.

In April 1943, a part of the Bergen-Belsen camp was taken over by the SS Economic-Administration Main Office, and two months later it was re-designated from a *Zivilinterniertenlager* (civilian internment camp), to an *Aufenthaltslager* (holding camp). Here in these two photographs is a typical quarters of an SS soldier or guard during this period. Note that the upper photograph shows Christmas decorations and a sign that reads 'SS War [time] Christmas 1939'.

A typical SS soldier's locker at his quarters. At Bergen-Belsen the guards had learned about enemies of the state, and had been given an in-depth indoctrination in SS philosophy and racial superiority. These ideological teachings were aimed at producing men who ardently believed in the new Aryan order. The SS guards had been infused with anti-Semitism. On the bulletin boards inside the SS barracks and canteen they often saw copies of the racist newspaper, *Der Stürmer*. These propaganda newspapers had deliberately been pinned up in order to reinforce racial hatred and violence.

SS soldiers at one of the many railway yards that were scattered across the Reich and Poland where prisoners including Jews arrived. They then disembarked, to be force-marched to the camps. Conditions onboard these trains were often horrific and as a consequence many died.

Two photographs showing SS guards at a sentry post. All of the guards at Bergen-Belsen were indoctrinated into an almost fanatical determination to serve the SS with blind allegiance. Commanding officers had invested each guard with the power of life and death over all the inmates of the camp. Rule breaking among the prisoners was classified as a crime, and guards were compelled to handout stringent punishments for disobedience.

SS guards relaxing in their quarters at Christmas. These guards had learnt to use their trade of brutality without the slightest compunction.

An SS guard walks through the compound of the camp in the summer of 1943. As an SS guard each man was compelled to implement orders to the prisoners with horrific efficiency. All SS guards were given extensive freedom to deal very harshly with any inmates they deemed to have committed a crime 'behind the wire'.

In the snow, and four photographs show SS guards at a training camp prior to the embarkation to a concentration camp. At Belsen, in addition to the general physical abuse meted out on the prisoners by the guards, the camp commandant often introduced other cruel punishments for these hapless individuals. Prisoners were deprived of warm food for up to four days, and were subjected to long periods of solitary confinement on a diet of bread and water.

SS troops rest in the compound of the camp in the summer of 1943. While off duty, guards were able to relax in the surroundings of the camp or visit the local towns and villages. Outside the camp they felt insulated from its brutality, and every SS man was determined to conceal as much of the gruesome knowledge as possible from the outside world.

SS guards at a training camp. To train as a camp guard each SS man was able to bury his emotions and become absorbed by camaraderie and loyalty to the SS. They saw their training in Germany and Poland as an education for the future. The SS offered each guard a clear example to follow. Trainees saw their first months in the concentration camp system as a first step in their careers in the SS.

Outside the camp SS commanding officers take pleasure in a game of cards while off duty. A female can be seen enjoying the warm weather laying on a bathing chair and smiling for the camera. During this period of the war it was not unusual for officers and their families to live in houses near to Belsen. In fact, a number of officers and their families were housed either in the centre of the town, or in the immediate vicinity of the main camp. They all enjoyed a far more comfortable lifestyle than they would have fighting on the frontline. It soon became a close-knit community where wives would visit each other, gossip, hold afternoon tea parties, and invite their husbands along for evening drinks and dinner. As for the children they would either attend private schools in the surrounding areas, or hire a governess.

In the vicinity of Belsen a commanding officer can be seen walking along a path. Behind him are SS guards marching in file with their bolt action rifles thrown over their right shoulders.

An off-duty SS guard can be seen with a little girl posing for the camera. Life for the SS was made as comfortable as possible. The guards often had the pleasure of knowing they could see their families and loved ones when off duty.

Here a photograph shows SS training. A number of young Germans were drafted directly into the concentration camp system. Many were appeared attracted by the nature of the duty involved, in spite of the fact that they did not know exactly what was in store for them, and once they were in training they soon lost any moral scruples about what they were required to do. For some that went to work at Belsen, it had given a chance to excel where their life had previously failed them.

An off-duty SS guard gives a cheeky smile for the camera. This image is a far cry from the arrogant overbearing manner in which most of the SS would be seen at Belsen. Often many would be seen beating, kicking, slapping, and whipping prisoners ruthlessly. They seemed to take great pride in the fact that their mere presence caused the inmates to tremble with fear. Gleefully each SS man followed the policy of controlled and disciplined terror laid down during their guard training.

An off-duty SS officer poses for the camera outside the camp. From the moment the SS personnel arrived in camp they inflicted pain and hardship on the new arrivals. The terror that ensued only generated further animosity and contempt towards both Soviet prisoners and Jews.

A smiling SS guard poses for the camera inside the camp compound. Many of the SS men that had come to Belsen, and indeed many of the other concentration camps, had considered their posting comfortable compared to being sent to the Eastern Front to fight the Red Army. Here the men lived in relative ease and were rewarded for meting out beatings and various forms of punishment. To be able to freely beat, brutalize and murder the prisoners it undoubtedly provided some the opportunity to compensate for feelings of inferiority. But there were those who struggled with the distressing sights of cold blooded murder.

Two photographs showing SS with their children. When the children were not attending school, they were looked after by domestic slaves who cooked meals and cleaned their nicely furnished homes. For the SS life was good, and when domestic products such as clothing and food became difficult to obtain they could usually be purchased from the ever-growing black market, or from the camp itself. Stealing and corruption was rife amongst the SS in the camp, and the black market was thriving. SS officers were personally benefiting from the accumulating wealth. Diamonds, gold, coins, foreign currency from all over Europe was stolen. Large amounts of food and alcohol too were taken for personal use and sold on the black market. Many items of clothing and furniture were pilfered by the SS as well.

Three photographs showing SS troops during a training exercise in the snow. The camp was heavily guarded around the perimeter of Belsen with sentry posts and machine gun or rifle positions at intervals. This made escaping for the inmates almost impossible. In the upper photograph, note the soldier using a Czech-built light machine gun, probably a ZB vz 30 model, one of the direct descendents of the British Bren gun.

Belsen locals enjoy a beer with an SS commanding officer. Behind this façade the SS men were hiding a terrible truth about their posting, and avoided ever uttering a single word about the killings outside the camp. As far as they were concerned the local inhabitants were not aware of the barbaric measures taken against the inmates in the camp.

An interesting photograph showing four off-duty SS guards posing for the camera inside the town. By associating themselves with the locals, it was often easier to suppress the feelings of guilt that any SS man may have felt.

Two photographs showing French POWs along with captured colonial troops being escorted along a road to the rear. Although their German captors treated most French soldiers humanely, colonial troops were not so lucky. When colonial soldiers surrendered they were often humiliated or beaten by German soldiers for having put up a fanatical resistance. However, the *SS-Totenkopf* (Death Head) frequently took no prisoners: North African troops they preferred to round up and have summarily shot on the spot.

Two photographs taken in sequence showing troops, probably from a reconnaissance battalion of the 8th Infantry Division, in a victory parade through Paris. In the background is the Arc de Triomphe de L'Étoile.

SS troops, more than likely from the 4th *SS-Polizei*, are seen in front of the Eiffel Tower. From this period on, the lives of Parisians and all those who lived in occupied France would change dramatically, none more so than those of the Jewish communities.

A column of troops march along a road. Littered across the roads and fields is the devastation caused by German forces as they push forward through France.

Chapter Two

Under *SS* Control

By the spring of 1943 the German war machine was suffering massive losses on the Eastern Front. Reverberations caused by the setback on the Eastern Front were increasingly being felt across the whole of Germany and occupied countries, in spite its ardent determination to win the war. Rolling stock for transporting large shipments of Jews by rail was causing major problems in some areas, for the armed forces desperately needed to move troops and other vital equipment from one part of the front to another as quickly as possible. While the 'Final Solution' accelerated at an even greater rate in the various killing centres of Poland, the need for a vast labour pool was a constant concern for the SS.

It was for this reason that the SS pressed the concentration camp system for more labour and ensuring that the camps were run more efficiently and profitably than ever before. In April 1943, a part of the Bergen-Belsen camp was taken over by the SS Economic-Administration Main Office. Initially the camp had been designated as a *Zivilinterniertenlager* or civilian internment camp. However, the SS re-designated Belsen as an *Aufenthaltslager* or holding camp. SS officials saw the potential of the camp where Jews could be transported and held there to be exchanged for German civilians interned in other countries, or for hard currency. The idea seemed a lucrative and effective means of increasing German man power for the front.

Within a couple of months the SS divided the camp into subsections for individual groups. There was a special camp for Polish Jews, a Hungarian camp, a neutrals camp for citizens of neutral countries, and a 'Star camp' for Dutch Jews. The POW camp known as Stalag XI-C was shut down and became a branch camp of Stalag XI-B. The SS saw the potential to make this part of the camp into a hospital for Russian POWs. Once they had recovered in the hospital they could be fed, set to work and eventually exchanged for money, or better still swapped for German POWs. The plan was fraught with internal problems, but nonetheless the hospital was opened and sick Russian POWs moved there. The SS gave the impression to the Geneva Convention that the camp was purely a holding area, and the inmates that were being cared for properly.

During the summer of 1943 thousands of Jews were transported to Belsen. Between then and December 1944 some 15,000 Jews, including 2,750 children and minors, were transported to the camp. With them they brought enormous quantities of food, money and jewels. All were taken from them, as well as a huge amount of alcoholic drink. This was distributed among the *SS* and *Wehrmacht* guards to be consumed when off duty in the barracks.

Generally the *SS* did not feel any sympathy towards one or other Jewish group from any particular country; however some *SS* men were confronted by a moral and emotional conflict when they received Western Jews, particularly from the 'Homeland'. They were able to identify with them much more easily than those from Poland and Russia. Unlike Eastern Jews whose religious, racial and national feelings were combined in one single identity, and had for centuries been ingrained in fear and terror from centuries of pogroms, Western Jews were recognized completely differently, as they had not suffered from years of pain and anguish. It was for this reason that the *SS* went to great lengths to mislead the Western Jews into believing they were being looked after. In some circumstances naivety of the Western Jews was such that some from the transport actually offered tips to those that were unloading them.

When they arrived through the gates they were greeted by the *SS* guards often in polite voices telling them to come through at their leisure, but in an orderly fashion. The *SS* wanted to make it as deceptive as possible tricking them into believing that they had reached a resettlement centre where they could rest before resuming their place of work and residence. The *SS* were shrewd in their understanding of the essential differences between Eastern and Western Jews, and this had become even more apparent during the last year of the war, as more people from the West arrived.

The early summer of 1943 had brought about an unusual atmosphere not seen in many other camps. This feeling was the direct result of the dire military situation on the Eastern Front and the fact the inmates had bargaining power. While *SS* rules in the camp were more stringent than ever before, there was also an underlying mood that some SS-men were becoming more relaxed, and forcing themselves to be slightly more affable with the inmates. As the prisoners were herded through into the camp for instance, the guards were ordered not to use whips or any type of physical abuse. However, once in the camp, the deception would be unmasked with guards hurling abuse and beating the prisoners for the least infringement of camp rules.

At the end of July 1943 the *Wehrmacht* in Russia had suffered permanent change. It now lacked the resources to conduct major offensive operations. The war had become nothing more for the average soldier than a long, bitter struggle to survive. With nothing but a string of defeats in its wake the German Army were now withdrawing across a devastated Soviet landscape, with little hope of holding back the Red Army. The summer campaign in Russia had been completely disastrous. Against overwhelming superiority the Germans withdrew some 150 miles along a 650 mile front.

Despite the new policies, the camp still grew in size as more and more Jews were transported through the system. To help oversee the inmates of the camp, women guards were drafted in. These women known as the *SS-Gefolge* were indoctrinated by their superior officers to hate the inmates, especially the Jewish prisoners. They were told to regard all prisoners as subhuman adversaries of the State, and those who offered the slightest resistance were marked for immediate destruction. Although most were not violently anti-Semitic at the time, they were told to consider the Jews the most dangerous of all the enemies of National Socialism.

Strolling around the camp wearing white brassards on their lower left tunic sleeves with a black cloth strip bearing the silver threaded *SS Aufseherin* stamp, a side cap distinctly displaying the infamous '*Totenkopf*' death head badge, together with military issue dress and wearing either hobnailed jack boots or black shoes with black socks, the female guards assisted their male counterparts in supervising the new arrivals, and their work detail.

Many new German women guards did not know what was actually in store for them. But once they were in training the prestige of the uniform, the elitism, the toughness and the comradeship soon overcame any morale scruples. Some apparently enjoyed meting out harsh and often brutal punishments for the slightest infractions of camp rules. Some were especially eager to show their SS superiors that they could be as brutal as their male counterparts.

Johanna Bormann was one of a handful of depraved and cruel women guards in the concentration camp. Even by SS standards, her behaviour was atrocious. Bormann would beat, kick, slap, and whip prisoners ruthlessly. She seemed to take great pride in the fact that her mere presence caused the inmates to tremble with fear. She gleefully followed the policy of controlled and disciplined terror laid down by the SS. With a nonchalant and cavalier attitude, this barbarous woman could conduct her cruel beatings without scruple.

Life for Bormann at Belsen was good; and even better was that she and her fellow comrades were able to steal from the dead. Surprisingly, the supervision of the SS members and female guards was actually loose. As a result there were so many causal opportunities to steal that it was hard to imagine that any of the SS members and female guards were free from involvement in this crime. From a female guard who wanted a new radio to the SS officer who dealt in stolen jewellery, corruption at the camps was endemic.

One of the most famous examples of corruption on a grand scale was that of Ilse Koch, known as 'the Bitch of Buchenwald'. She was the chief female guard at the Buchenwald camp, and married to the camp commandant, Karl Koch. Both embezzled large sums of money and afforded themselves free range of the inmates' belongings; there is also evidence that the Kochs had the witnesses to their misdeeds murdered.

When Johanna Bormann was transferred from Auschwitz to Bergen-Belsen in late 1944 she had packed her suitcase containing not only her belongings, but stolen jewellery and money in various currencies. Journeying to Belsen she hoped the fruits of a new camp would yield further temptations. As soon as Johanna arrived she was assigned immediately to roll call duties. Some weeks later her immediate superior, Irma Grese arrived. Grese had come from Auschwitz where her name was synonymous with brutality. In 1943, aged 20, she was transferred from Ravensbrück to Auschwitz, where she became *Oberaufseherin*, controlling thirty-one barracks housing some 30,000 women. Although she had mistreated prisoners at Ravensbrück, Auschwitz afforded her much greater opportunities for doing evil. Tidy and immaculately groomed, she strutted around the camp with her black boots, whip, and smart looking SS uniform looking for victims she could torture or kill. At Belsen she was determined to inflict the same misery. The Belsen commandant, Kramer, had already reassigned Grese, but she asked him if she could stay. Kramer, a man who was reputed to be one of her many lovers, authorized Grese to have her permanent assignment at Belsen. To her female colleagues it seemed that SS matron Grese wanted to remain at the typhus-ridden hell-hole just for the love of her SS boyfriend. Yet, as Johanna Bormann soon found out, Irma was in fact secretly having an affair with an SS guard who she referred always as 'her Hatchi'. Hatchi was in fact *SS-Oberscharführer* Franz Hatzinger. Hatzinger and Grese had met each other while they were stationed at Auschwitz. He was a married man and fourteen years older than Grese, but it was clear to Johanna that they both were very close and regularly sneaked off secretly to have sex.

Another female guard at Belsen who wanted to stay for the love of another SS guard was Elisabeth Volkenrath. Her opportunity to stay at Belsen, like Grese, would ultimately put her own life in jeopardy as the allies fast approached from the west. But both women had decided to stay, whatever the outcome. In spite the deteriorating military situation the women continued to inflict the same sort of terror and cruelty they had become notorious for at Auschwitz. Prisoners were dying all around them and typhus was rife throughout the camp, but Grese and Volkenrath would order frail, emaciated prisoners to undergo strenuous exercises, including making inmates hold heavy rocks over their heads for extended periods of time.

(*Opposite*) A group photo of SS guards smile for the camera. For these new SS recruits entering the realms of the concentration camp system, camp duty was a way of testing their inner beliefs. They had learned about enemies of the state, and been given an in-depth indoctrination in SS philosophy. These ideological teachings were aimed at producing men who ardently believed in the new Aryan order.

Four photographs showing SS Police squads during operations in the Soviet Union in 1943. In the eyes of the SS the Soviet Union represented the home of Bolshevism and international Jewry, which needed to be rooted out and destroyed. To deal with the Jews in Russia there were four *Einsatzgruppen* (Action Groups) consisting of *Sipo-SD* personnel, *Waffen-SS* units, and police. Progress through the Soviet heartlands was swift and a bloodbath against the Jewish population ensued. When the SS were not murdering, they were rounding up Jews and sending them to the rear where they would be transported either to various ghettos across Europe or direct to labour or death camps.

Two photographs showing *Totenkopf* troops out on the front line in Russia. It was the *Totenkopfverbände* – Death's Head units of the *SS* which were deployed to guard concentration camps. Throughout the war, in spite of the military arm of the *Totenkopf* fighting on the battlefield, the *Totenkopf* still retained close ties to the concentration camp service. Its members continued to wear the Death's Head as their unit insignia, and were known to be brutal both on and off the battlefield, a result of the original doctrine of 'no pity' which Eicke had instilled in his camp personnel as far back as 1934. Theodore Eicke was the fanatical commander of the 3rd *SS* Panzer Division *Totenkopf* until he was killed.

An SS soldier guards the entrance to a camp. Security at these camps was tight, and fear of someone escaping was constant among the commandants that ran the camps. In Germany many of the camps, such as Bergen-Belsen, were believed to be 'holding camps' purely to temporarily detain Jews. Many German civilians did not believe, or chose not to believe, that thousands were perishing through institutionalised murder.

An SS guard in the vicinity of the camp rests on a bench. These guards were ordered to be brutal with the Jews and use whatever violence was necessary to keep them in check.

At Bergen-Belsen food was abundant for the guards, but fresh food such as meat was something of a luxury. However, locals of the town sometimes sold chickens to the men in the camp. Here off-duty staff of the camp prepare chickens for an evening meal.

An SS man poses for the camera with his loved one while off duty. The personnel at Bergen-Belsen could visit loved ones and family when off duty. They found that a posting there was relatively easy, and had as much food and alcohol to drink as they wanted.

An SS soldier poses for the camera with smiling nurses on the front line. By mid-1943 the military reversal in the East was causing severe logistical problems. The rolling stock used for transporting large shipments of Jews by rail was causing major problems in some areas, for the armed forces desperately needed to move troops and other vital equipment from one part of the front to another as quickly as possible. But despite the inconvenience caused by the continuing war, thousands of Jews were still evacuated and successfully transported from all over Europe and the East and subjected to what the Nazis referred to as 'special treatment'.

A portrait photograph of a newly recruited SS guard. Often photographs like this were sent back home to family or loved ones, and regularly took pride of place in the domestic home.

SS men grouped around a vehicle. By mid-1943 the war in the East looked like it would be a prolonged battle of attrition. The Reich was now suffering shortages of men and material, and the concentration camp administration was torn between mass killings and trying to retain manpower for slave labour.

(*Opposite*) Troops on the Eastern Front during the winter of 1943. During the winter months of 1943 both the *Wehrmacht* and the *Waffen-SS* had suffered unimaginable casualties and huge losses of equipment. Nearly 600 miles of the front had stagnated, with some battles being fought out in conditions similar to those of the First World War. From the frozen Baltic, around the city of Leningrad, south to Lake Ilmem, across the vast tall pine forest of the Rzhev salient, and then down to Orel, German forces had hardly moved in twelve bitter months of fighting. The high command of the SS had known that during Germany's early victories they had little to fear in the implementation of continent-wide deportations of Jews. Ethnic cleansing was undoubtedly influenced to a certain degree by the military situation, and it was this military success that fed the SS lust for more Jewish blood. So it might be expected that military difficulties would diminish the Nazi's endless desire for wide-spread deportations of Jews – but they did not.

Two SS men on leave in Berlin in the summer of 1943. One of the harder matters for an SS guard, especially somewhere like Belsen, was dealing with German and Austrian Jews. But the majority of SS personnel were not emotionally disturbed by these shipments from their country, and had developed a capacity for dissociating themselves from it to some extent.

Off-duty SS men play on the ice during the late winter of 1943; a stark contrast with the horrors of the camp and the treatment they were inflicting on its inmates.

(*Opposite*) A portrait photograph showing an SS man and a member of the Afrika Korps posing together in a group photograph in 1942. By this period of the war hundreds of concentration camps had been erected across Germany and the occupied countries.

A guard on duty around the perimeter of the camp in the freezing snow. He wears a toque protecting his face from the extreme winter conditions. The inmates inside the camp had no additional protection from the weather, and the cold often killed the sick, the old, and young children.

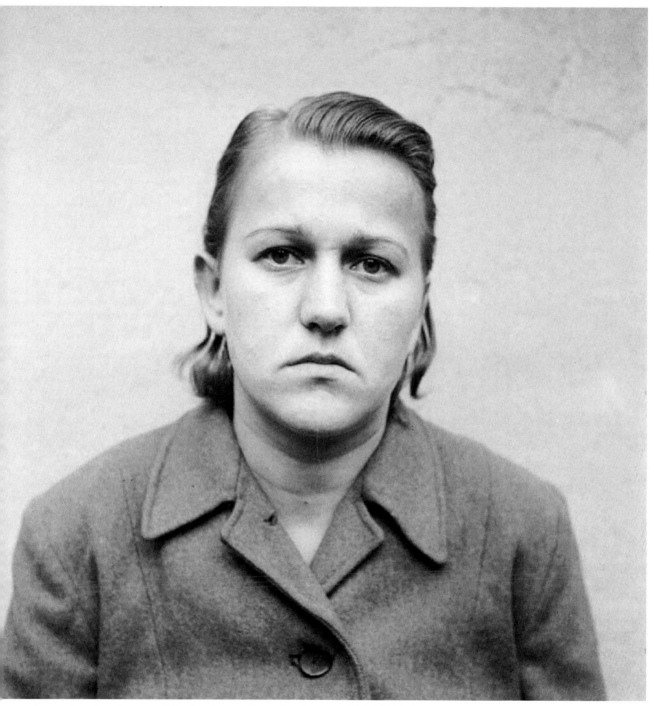

A mug shot showing one of the female guards running the camp. This is Hilde Liesewitz. The code of conduct for these female guards was based upon the SS demand for blind and absolute obedience to all orders from SS superior officers, and upon their insistence that each prisoner be treated with great brutality as an enemy of the state. Exhorting the women guards to constantly hate the prisoners, and simultaneously buttressing this hatred with the legality of orders, enabled the guards to mete out the harshest punishments to the prisoners. (*Imperial War Museum, BU-9693*)

A mug shot of Wilhelm Dörr. Before going to Belsen Dörr had been a concentration camp guard at Sachsenhausen. In January 1944 Dörr was transferred to the Mittelbau-Dora concentration camp where he became *Blockführer* (Block Leader) in the central camp complex before being appointed deputy to *Hauptscharführer* Franz Stofel, commander of the sub-camp of Kleinbodungen. As the war was coming to an end Dörr was one of forty-five guards that led a horrific death march from Mittelbau-Dora to Bergen-Belsen. He had only been at the camp for four days when Belsen was liberated. He was one of many indicated for various atrocities. He later stood before a British military court in Lüneburg as part of the so-called Belsen Trials, was found guilty, and hanged for war crimes in December 1945. (*Imperial War Museum, BU-9721*)

A photograph of Hilde Lobauer, a female guard at Belsen. She had been sent to Ravensbrück concentration camp as a prisoner, where she stayed until March 1942. She was then transferred to Auschwitz where she was ordered to work in the camp as an *Arbeitsdienstführerin*. However, when the Russians began advancing through Poland in January 1945 she left the camp and went back to Ravensbrück, where she stayed for four weeks, and then accompanied a transport to Belsen, where she arrived in March 1945. Kommandant Kramer made her *Arbeitsdienstführerin* again.
(*Imperial War Museum, BU-6357*)

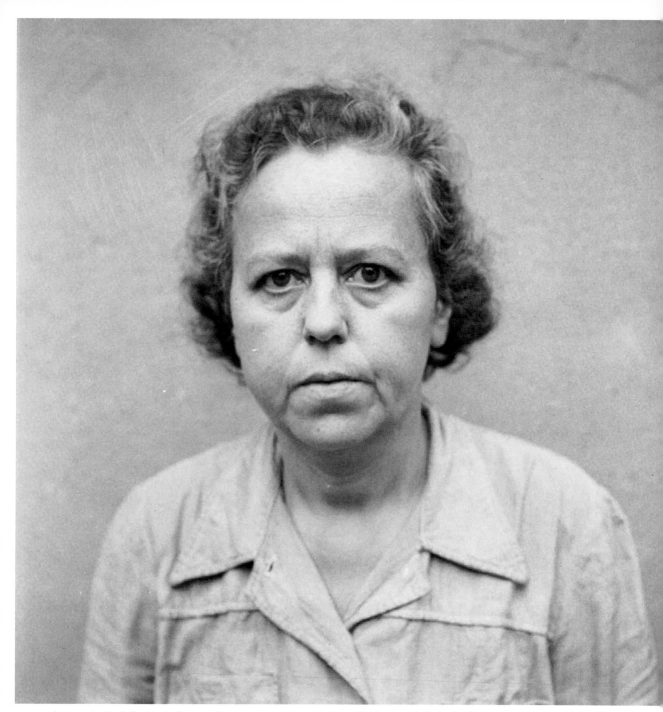

A mug shot of Gertrude Saurer. She was conscripted in late 1944 as an *Aufseherin*. She was a guard at Gross Rosen and then moved to Langenbielau. On 8 November she went to a factory in Roersdorf as *Lagerführerin* to oversee prisoners. They were then evacuated and on 28th February 1945 arrived at Belsen. Saurer worked in the bath houses and kitchens, and enjoyed meting out harsh and brutal punishments for the slightest infractions of camp rules. *(Imperial War Museum, BU-6680)*

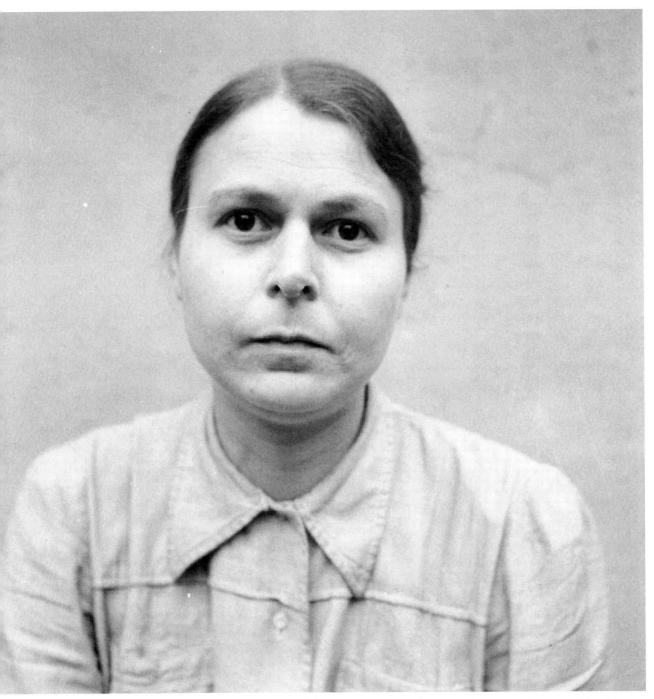

Aufseherin Gertrude Feist. By 1943, the Reich Labour Ministry was empowered to conscript women between 17 and 45 years of age for labour service, and by the end of that year, most of the women reporting for concentration camp training were conscripts. Almost immediately when Feist became an *Aufseherin* she was told by her superior officers to hate the inmates, especially the Jewish prisoners. She was told to regard all prisoners as subhuman adversaries of the state, and those who offered the slightest resistance were marked for immediate destruction. *(Imperial War Museum, BU-968)*

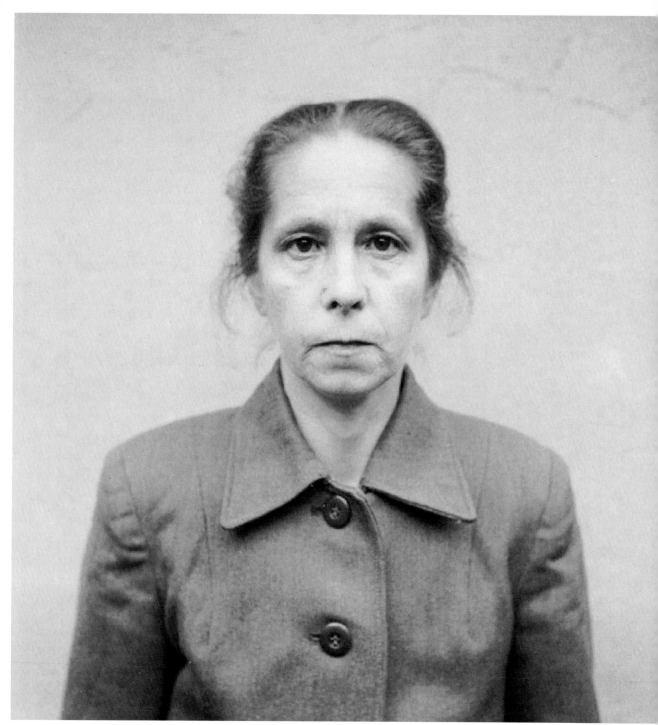

Johanna Bormann photographed before her trial. When Johanna was transferred from Auschwitz to Bergen-Belsen in late 1944 she had packed her suitcase containing not only her own belongings, but stolen jewellery and money in various currencies. Journeying to Bergen-Belsen she hoped the fruits of a new camp would yield further pickings. Johanna was assigned immediately to roll call duties. It did not take her long before she started taking great pride in the fact that her mere presence caused the inmates to tremble with fear. Quite often she was seen unleashing her 'big bad wolfhound' (German shepherd) on helpless prisoners, or beating them with a stick or truncheon, sometimes killing them in the process. *(Imperial War Museum, BU-9682)*

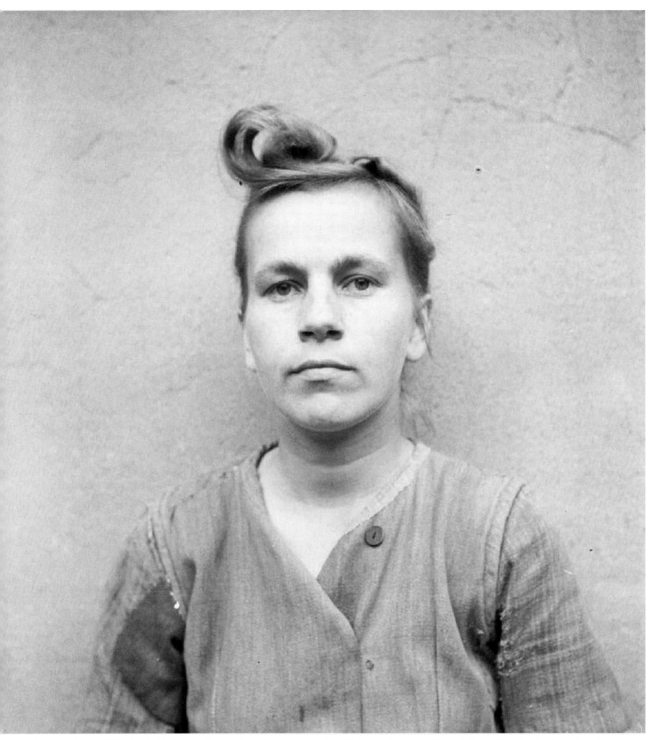

A mug shot of Elisabeth Volkenrath, another female guard at Belsen, also transferred from Auschwitz. In spite the deteriorating military situation the women continued to inflict the same sort of terror and cruelty they had become notorious for at Auschwitz. Volkenrath and her fellow guards would order frail, emaciated prisoners to undergo strenuous exercises, including making them hold heavy rocks over their heads for extended periods of time. In love with another SS guard, as the allies fast approached from the west, she decided to stay whatever the outcome. She was executed for war crimes in December 1945. (*Imperial War Museum, BU-9689*)

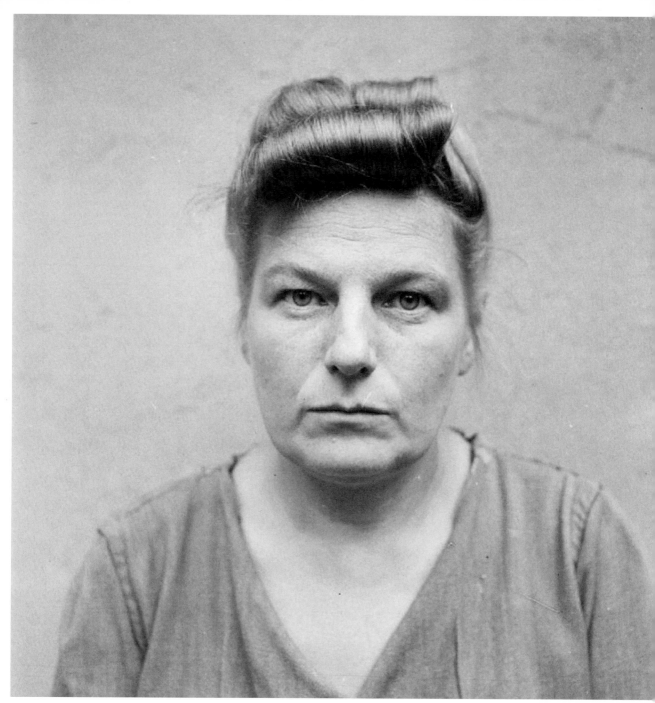

A photograph of Herta Ehlert. Despite the pending collapse of the Third Reich, the majority of the women guards including Ehlert did not attempt to prepare themselves for inevitable post war retribution. Even as the audible sounds of enemy gun fire became louder with each passing day, most of the women, unlike their male counterparts, never tried to gain favour with the inmates by treating them better, even when it was clear to them that Germany would lose the war. (*Imperial War Museum, BU-9690*)

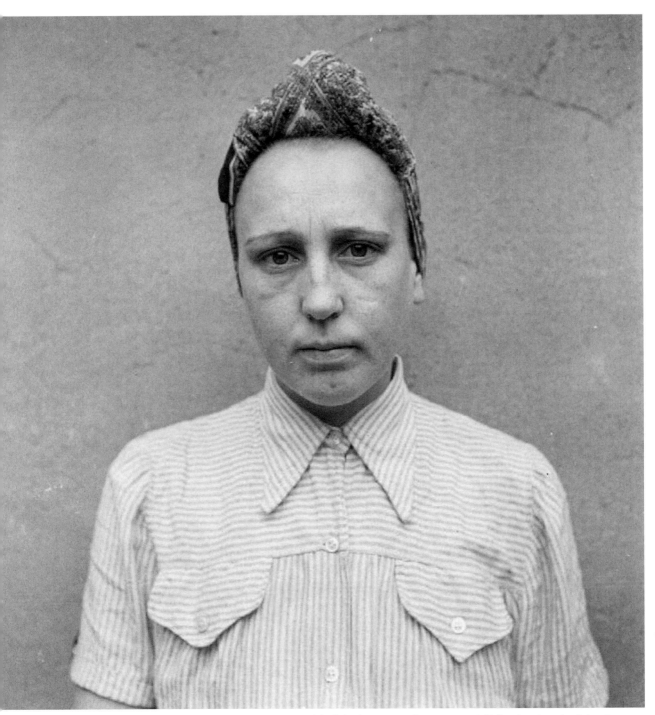

Aufseherin Frieda Walter first started working in Kitchen No. 3 in the women's compound. Following that she joined the '*Kiesel Kommando*' overseeing inmates moving stones. She then joined the garden Kommando in the garden of the commandant, where she beat and terrorised the inmates. *(Imperial War Museum, BU-9695)*

The 'beautiful beast'. A mug shot of the infamous Irma Grese. This young female guard was synonymous with inflicting various forms of brutality on the inmates. Hardened from working at Auschwitz she came to Belsen and immediately retained her barbaric reputation. Strutting around the camp with her black boots, whip, and smart looking SS uniform, she regularly looked for victims she could torture or kill. Irma's sadistic enjoyment of torture and murder eventually saw her being sent to the gallows in December 1945 for her crimes against humanity. (*Imperial War Museum, BU-9700*)

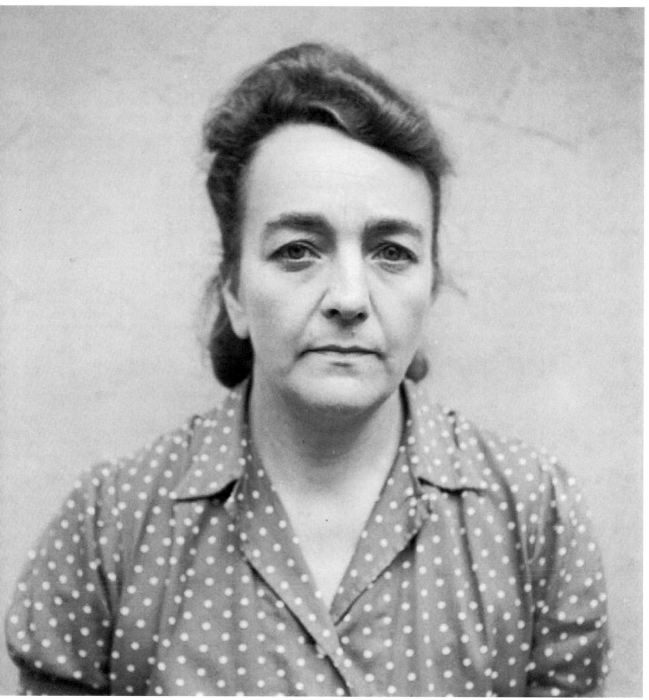

Aufseherin Anna Hempel was conscripted into the SS in May 1944 and sent to Ravensbrück. Within a few weeks she was evacuated to Guben, and then soon after moved to Bergen-Belsen, reaching there on 17 February 1945. At Belsen she oversaw the inmates in the bath-house and Kitchen No. 2 in the men's compound. (*Imperial War Museum, BU-9702*)

SS-Hauptsturmführer commandant Josef Kramer. In December 1944, Kramer was transferred from Birkenau to Bergen-Belsen where he was promoted commandant. Kramer's rule was so barbaric that he became known as the 'Beast of Belsen'. Even as the Reich became squeezed by the advance of both Soviet and Allied troops, and the administration of the camp broke down, Kramer remained devoted to bureaucracy and continued his reign of terror on the inmates. As a result of his unrestrained barbarity, many thousands starved to death. *(Imperial War Museum, BU-9711)*

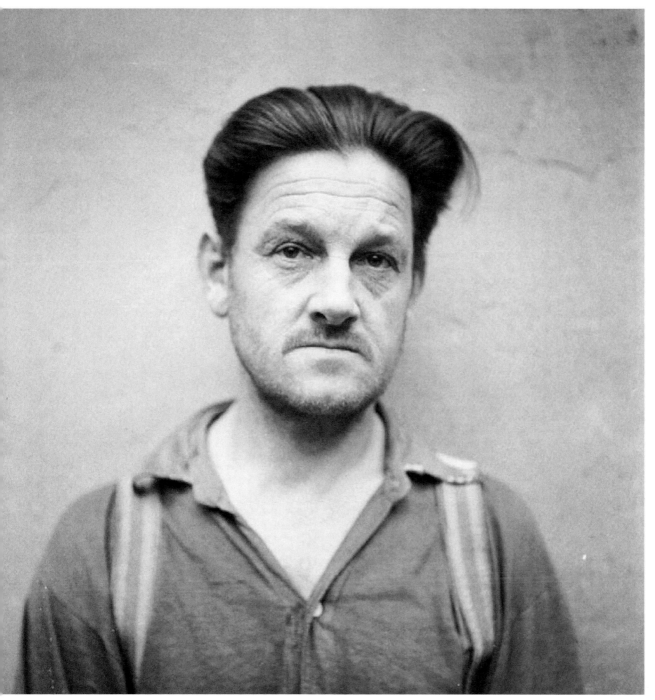

SS-Obersturmführer Franz Hössler was Protective Custody Leader at the Auschwitz-Birkenau, Dora-Mittelbau and Bergen-Belsen concentration camps. On 8 April 1945, Hössler arrived with his transport at Bergen-Belsen and became deputy camp commander under Josef Kramer. There he would shoot many prisoners, and continued this habit right up until the day the camp was liberated. *(Imperial War Museum, BU-9714)*

Vladislav Ostrowski was a conscripted concentration camp guard who was sent by train with a transport which left Dora on 2 April 1945 and arrived in Belsen on the 10th. Ostrowski was put in Block 26, but then fell ill and was sent to Block 19. This block was attached to the hospital and he remained there until the British troops arrived. (*Imperial War Museum, BU-9730*)

Ignatz Schlomovicz, a female concentration camp guard at Belsen. (*Imperial War Museum, BU-9731*)

Kapo Erich Zoddel was transferred to Bergen-Belsen on 27 March 1944 and took up quarters in Block 4 (part of the *Häftlingslager*). Zoddel was a sadistic murderer and was often seen around the camp beating and torturing the inmates. (*Imperial War Museum, BU-9726*)

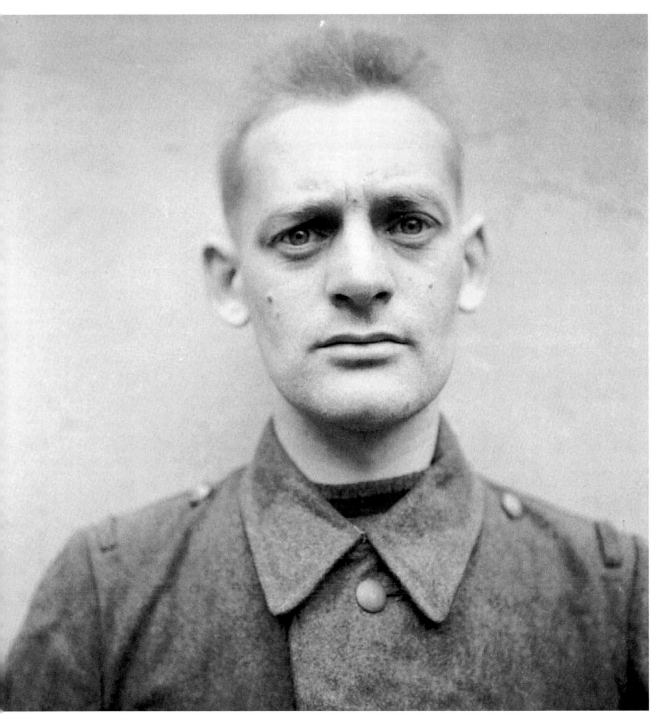

SS Hauptscharführer Franz Xaver Stöfel perpetrated extreme acts of brutality and blood lust at Belsen. Stöfel was one of the most depraved and cruel *SS* men in the concentration camp. He was often seen beating, kicking, and whipping prisoners mercilessly. On occasions he would kill them in cold blood for the least infraction of camp rules. (*Imperial War Museum, BU-9740*)

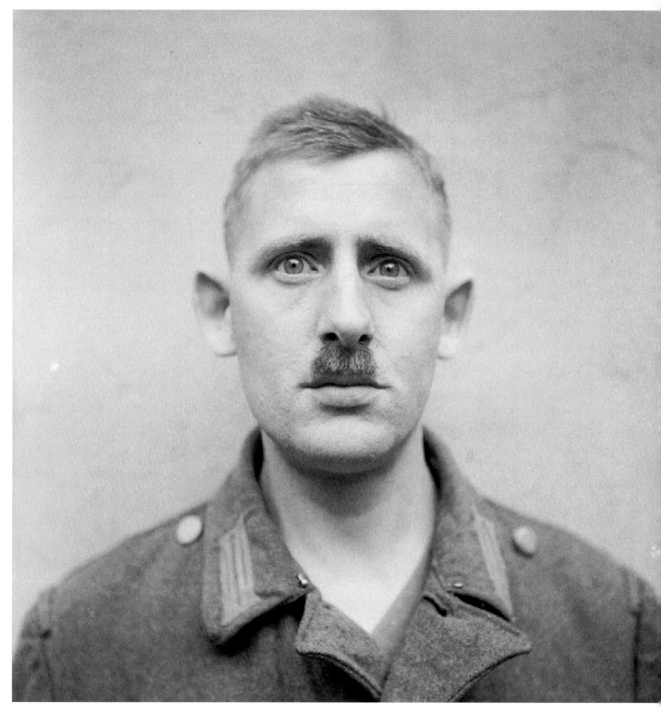

Ausgar Pichen gleefully followed the policy of controlled and disciplined terror at Belsen. During his short stay at the camp he became synonymous among the inmates with inflicting various forms of brutality without showing any pity for them whatsoever. (*Imperial War Museum, BU-9741*)

SS troops stand in front of some rolling stock. By this period of the war the rail system was desperately required for the war effort and this inevitably caused problems with transportation of shipments to the concentration camp system.

Waffen-SS troops are preparing to be moved to another area on the Eastern Front. Whilst the German war machine frantically attempted to hold its troops on the front lines on an overextended front, elsewhere the Nazi hierarchy were continuing with their mission of moving millions of people through the concentration camp system and having them worked to death or murdered.

Three photographs showing *Wehrmacht* troops fighting during the winter, trying in vain to hold off the advancing enemy troops. As the Western and Eastern Fronts shrunk, more and more concentration camps fell to the onrushing enemy forces.

Inside a German town and *Waffen-SS* troops prepare their meagre defences against an overwhelming enemy. Both the Russians and Allied forces were now fighting their way across the Reich meeting heavy resistance. By this period many of the concentration camps had fallen into enemy hands. However, lots of the camps were evacuated before the enemy arrived and the weak and starving prisoners sent on long death marches to other camps, notably Belsen.

Defending the Reich was key to the last ditch defence. Here a soldier lays a mine.

A 2cm FlaK 38 gun unit halted on a railway flat-bed car during the last months of the defence of the Reich. Whilst many the soldiers at the end of the war tried to dissociate themselves with having any knowledge of the concentration camp system, many of them were aware of their existence.

A long column of German vehicles pours across the Russian border during the beginning of the German invasion of the Soviet Union on 22 June 1941. Following in the rear of the *Wehrmacht* advance was the notorious *Einsatzgruppen*, which rounded up and murdered those they regarded as hostile to the Reich, including the entire Jewish population.

Two SS concentration camp men are seen together. In April 1943 Belsen was taken over by the SS Economic Administration Office. The SS re-designated the camp as a holding camp.

SS troops out in the field on the Eastern Front during 1943. By this period of the war the German war machine was suffering massive losses. Rolling stock for transporting large shipments of Jews by rail was causing major problems in some areas for the fighting forces that needed to move vital equipment to the front.

An SS artillery crew during operations in the summer of 1943. It was during this time that thousands of Jews were being transported to Belsen.

An SS *Nebelwerfer* crew preparing for action somewhere on the Eastern Front in the winter of 1943.

SS guards smoke and drink while off duty. The SS saw Belsen as a lucrative investment where they could hold Jews in the camp to be exchanged for German civilians in other countries, or for hard currency.

An SS Tiger tank of the *Leibstandarte* rolls along a road bound for the battlefront.

SS Panther tanks are parked in a farm. Note the application of foliage to prevent detection from the air.

Two Panther tanks on the battlefield pass each other.

An SS StuG belonging to the *Polizei*-Division somewhere on the Eastern Front.

Wehrmacht troops cross a river during fighting on the Eastern Front.

During the summer of 1943 German soldiers have time to wash and relax next to a transport train used for rolling stock of Jews.

Two camouflaged vehicles parked outside a camp in Germany in the winter of 1943.

Western Jews are being escorted along a road by German troops in the summer of 1943. During this period thousands of Jews were transported to Belsen. Between then and December 1944 some 15,000 Jews, including 2,750 children and minors, were deported to the camp. *(Bartek Zborksi)*

A group of Jews have been rounded up in a square ready for deportation to a camp. *(Bartek Zborksi)*

Jews have been rounded up and prepared for transportation to a concentration camp. Due to the lack of rolling stock being used for vast shipments of other Jews across Europe and for military use, this particular shipment has used standard railway carriages for transportation.

A photograph taken of local Nazis in the town of Belsen, taken probably before the camp was built. After the war many of the locals said that they had not known about the camp and what terrible atrocities had occurred there.

SS guards pose for the camera sometime in 1942.

A group of SS men are seen conferring with each other.

SS men probably from a nearby training camp pose for the camera under a road sign.

A group of SS men pose for the camera.

A group photograph showing a Police unit which was responsible for rounding up Jews and sending them to concentration camps. *(Bartek Zborksi)*

An SS commanding officer is seen inside the rear of a vehicle handing out something to his men.

A portrait photograph of the notorious Belsen commandant Josef Kramer taken before his command at the camp.
(*Bartek Zborksi*)

Viennese Jews being rounded up from their homes by German authorities to be deported to destinations like Belsen.
(*Bartek Zborksi*)

Three photographs showing the plight of the Jewish community under Nazi administration during the war. Two of the photographs clearly show the arm bands worn by the Jews with the Star of David.

Chapter Three

Liberation

During the last months of the war the situation for the Germans was dire. They had fought desperately to maintain cohesion and hold their positions in battles that often saw thousands perish. By the early spring of 1945 their overstretched and undermanned armies were fighting on German soil both on the eastern and western fronts, against the overwhelming strength of the enemy. To make matters worse troop units were no longer being refitted with replacements to compensate for the large losses sustained. Most soldiers were all too aware that they were in the final stages of the war.

By this period of the war many of the concentration camps and death camps had already fallen into enemy hands. In those camps not yet captured there was unease and deep concern amongst the guards. Some struggled psychologically with the daily duties of murder and many stayed on as obedient subordinates, driven perhaps by the 'banality of evil'. At Belsen, the majority of the SS were not ideologically motivated, nor were they Nazi fanatics perverted by torture and death. The job to them was simply a way for them to survive in the realms of the SS order, however evil their task was.

Even as the war neared its end in April 1945, both the female and male guards continued upholding their mission to eliminate Nazi-designated sub-humanity from the face of the earth. But despite the pending collapse of the Third Reich, the majority of the women guards did not attempt to prepare themselves for the inevitable post war retribution. Even as the audible sounds of enemy gun fire became louder with each passing day, most of the women, unlike their male counterparts, never tried to gain favour with the inmates by treating them better, even when it was clear to them that Germany would lose the war. With the advance of British forces into the area, the female guards remained at their posts.

The advance units of the British Second Army that liberated Bergen-Belsen on the 15 April were not psychologically prepared for what they encountered when they arrived at the gates of the camp that day. British soldiers were numbed and nauseated by what they saw, smelled, and heard. They were also amazed when they approached the main gate in a motorised column: they found that the SS personnel, as if preparing for a formal reception, were drawn up in their field grey uniforms. The

SS guards appeared cheerful. Josef Kramer for instance seemed unusually outgoing, friendly, and pleasant. Yet behind them were 10,000 unburied dead, in addition to mass graves which already contained 40,000 more corpses. At that time as many as 500 a day were perishing from the long-term effects of starvation and the resultant diseases. Yet he appeared more concerned that the British would use their loud-speakers, fearing it might cause the inmates to stampede. Then, as the British moved further into the camp, the sound of periodic small arms fire could be heard: SS guards were firing on inmates surging towards the kitchen in the hope of finding something to eat. Irma Grese attacked a British General as he was attempting to enter some huts, but she was immediately restrained. After many of the SS personnel were taken into custody, Kramer spoke of the starving masses as if he were referring to cattle.

When the British came upon the women guards' compound, the troops were confronted by a formation of well-fed, overweight, female guards who were said to be casually standing around chatting and smoking cigarettes waiting for their conquerors. One soldier recalled that many of the women had contorted, ugly facial expressions and all wore either hobnailed jack boots or military issue dress shoes with black socks.

Once the SS women were arrested, they joined the men on burial details. All of them had the gruesome task of dragging corpses to the pits. The soldiers noticed that the majority of the women reacted differently to this ghastly work than the men did. While some of the men ran away from the ordeal and one committed suicide, none of the women attempted to avoid it.

Walking around the camp, British troops were numbed by the appalling condition of the inmates. Lieutenant-Colonel R.I.G. Taylor, the Commanding Officer of the 63rd Anti-Tank Regiment, recalled his impressions of the camp at liberation:

> A great number of them [the inmates] were little more than living skeletons with haggard yellowish faces. Most of the men wore a striped pyjama type of clothing others wore rags, while women wore striped flannel gowns or any other clothing they had managed to acquire. Many of them were without shoes and wore only socks and stockings. There were men and women lying in heaps on both sides of the track. Others were walking slowly and aimlessly about – a vacant expression on their starved faces.

The British found 40,000 prisoners still alive at the time of the camp's liberation and almost immediately commenced efforts to save the sick and starving. The Deputy Director of Medical Services for the British Second Army, Brigadier H.L. Glyn-Hughes, was to oversee the mammoth task of aiding and feeding them and preventing the spread of infectious diseases.

To further help the relief effort the British allowed the Hungarians to remain in charge and only commandant Kramer was arrested. However, some of the Hungarian guards with their SS counterparts murdered some of the starving prisoners who attempted to get into the store houses. As a result of this the British supervised and guarded the food supplies and started to provide direct emergency medical care, clothing and food. The water supply too was reestablished after departing German soldiers had sabotaged the water supply in the barracks.

While many of the inmates were too sick or weak to do anything but lay down in their own filth, there were some stronger prisoners that were capable of undertaking revenge killings. This was particularly the case in the satellite camp known as the Hohne-Camp. Some 15,000 prisoners from Mittelbau-Dora had been marched under horrendous conditions and relocated there in early April. Mittelbau-Dora had been a sub-camp of Buchenwald concentration camp. Its prisoners had been worked to death by the SS mainly in the tunnel excavation situated near Nordhausen, where the V-2 rocket and the flying bomb V-1 rocket were produced. Life for the inmates there was terrible. Summary executions, deliberately being starved, and extreme cruelty were quite normal occurrences there. However, with the advancing Allied forces approaching Dora, the SS murdered those too sick to be marched, and those strong enough were put on a death march to the Hohne-Camp. While the SS continued to beat, starve and murder them in their new camp, many of the inmates were in much better physical condition than those in the main Belsen camp. After its liberation on 15 April 1945 some of the stronger prisoners turned on those who had been their overseers at Mittelbau. Some 170 of these *Kapos* were murdered in revenge killings.

Elsewhere in the camp, the surviving prisoners were fed slowly and given water. A delousing station was erected, and once deloused the recovering inmates were moved to a nearby German Panzer army camp, which became the Bergen-Belsen DP camp. For the next month, thousands of survivors were moved to the Panzer army camp.

In the meantime, while the living were being kept alive, the dead were being planned for mass burial in huge pits. Though most of the documents and adminis-trative files were destroyed by the SS before the handover of the camp, the British were determined not only to film and photograph what they witnessed as evidence of what the Germans had done, but were determined to force the remaining SS personnel under armed guard to bury the dead in pits. Burying the dead was an insult to the SS and their female counterparts, but it was a way of degrading them for their heinous crimes, and making them in some way accountable for their actions.

As the dead were being buried the typhus epidemic and louse infestation con-tinued to spread through Belsen at an alarming rate, causing more deaths. As a result of this the British drew up plans to burn the camp once everyone had been moved to the Hohne-Camp. Over a period of a month some 29,000 people were moved into the new camp. British troops then moved flame-throwing Bren gun carriers and Churchill Crocodile tanks into Belsen and burned the camp to the ground.

In spite the efforts of the British to help the remaining survivors with food and medical aid, a further 14,000 people died between the time of the liberation in April and the end of June 1945.

As for the perpetrators of the crimes of Belsen – Josef Kramer, Irma Grese, Elisabeth Volkenrath, and Johanna Bormann – all finally received retribution for their deeds. But following their 'Belsen Trial' in November 1945 they had gone to the gallows never regretting their heinous crimes against humanity. Ultimately their only regret as they walked to the gallows was that the Fatherland had lost the war. In their minds, they had acted in accordance with orders and had done their job to the best of their ability. During their murderous career they had sent thousands of people to their deaths. Yet, they never really thought that what they had done was wrong. Contrary to popular belief, most of the guards did not have a robot-like obedience that accounted for their ability to commit so many inhumane acts. Neither were they were natural born killers, but over time killers is what they learnt and chose to become.

As concentration camp guards they generally performed their work with enthusiasm and took pride in their achievements. Like so many other guards these people were able to bury their emotions and their natural revulsion at committing atrocities because the Jews were regarded as 'the enemy' and had no intrinsic right to life. Unravelling the complex motivation of people like Kramer or Grese lies not in the person, but the ideas that possessed them. Their willingness to subject people to physical suffering because they had been ordered to do so has long been dismissed as a valid legal defence. At places like Belsen they were educated in death and brutality, which they themselves put into practice. They had chosen to put what they had learned into operation, with devastating results. They were undoubtedly willing accomplices to murdering huge numbers of innocent men, women and children.

Germans troops defending their positions against the enemy's advance in January/ February 1945. In the last months of the war German forces continued to retreat across a scarred and devastated wasteland. On both the Western and Eastern Fronts, the last agonising moments of the war were played out. As the Russians advanced through Poland hundreds of thousands of concentration camp inmates, those strong enough to stand, were force-marched across Poland into Germany, many of them going to the already overcrowded camp of Belsen.

A German defensive position somewhere along the front lines. Here troops have deployed a 10.5cm artillery piece beside a building during the last months of the war in 1945.

Waffen-SS troops defending a position somewhere on the Western Front in Germany in March 1945. A 2cm FlaK gun is used in a ground attack against advancing enemy troops.

A tank commander scours the terrain using a pair of binoculars from the turret of his Panther. While German troops were feverishly trying to defend ground against the rapid progress of the Anglo-American advance, concentration camps across the Reich were either being evacuated, dismantled or destroyed. The dire military situation caused a number of camps not yet under threat from falling into enemy hands to become over-populated with additional inmates, which greatly increased the rate of dying through disease or starvation. Belsen was one such camp.

A German artillery unit unloading ammunition from a supply train. By this period much of the German rail network was either in enemy hands or destroyed. What lines were left, were used entirely for moving vital supplies to one part of the collapsing front to another. For the concentration camp system, inmates that were being evacuated from one camp to another were seldom allowed rail access and were forced on long foot marches, which were often referred to as 'death marches'.

On 15 April 1945 the British Army arrives at Belsen concentration camp. A Comet tank of the 11th Armoured Division passes the camp gate. As British troops advanced towards Belsen on 11 April *SS Reichsführer* Heinrich Himmler agreed to have the camp handed over without a fight. *SS* guards ordered prisoners to bury some of the dead. The next day, *Wehrmacht* representatives negotiated with British forces, and an agreement was signed, designating an area of nineteen square miles around the camp as a neutral zone. Ironically, most of the *SS* in the camp, including those billeted inside the town of Belsen with their families, were allowed to leave. *(Imperial War Museum, BU-3928)*

(*Opposite*) Posing for the camera is a group of *Wehrmacht* troops in a forest somewhere in Germany in April 1945. Despite the overwhelming advance of the Anglo-American forces through Germany, German troops were still fighting aggressively, trying in vain to hold onto their hopeless positions before the final collapse of the Reich. In fact, British forces were unable to get to Belsen as planned on 14 April as the surrounding area was still heavily guarded by Hungarian and *Wehrmacht* troops. It would not be until the next day that they finally arrived.

A British soldier speaks to one of the many inmates left starving in the camp. When the British and Canadian troops finally entered Belsen, they found thousands of unburied bodies. Including the satellite camps, there were at least 53,000 dead inmates. These were harrowing scenes for the troops that entered the camp, and they were appalled by what the Germans had done. (*Imperial War Museum, BU-4002*)

British troops have rounded up some of the remaining SS guards in the camp and go through their identity papers. Some of the guards attempted to disguise themselves as prisoners, but were either pointed out in selections by the inmates, or were detected by British troops because of their healthy and well-fed appearance. (*Imperial War Museum, BU-3928*)

A photograph of part of the camp, showing the inside perimeter of the fence topped with barbed wire and overlooked by wooden watch towers. *(National Archives)*

One of the many children that died in Belsen from disease and starvation. Because of the huge flood of new arrivals the SS could not cope. Not only were the prisoners dying of starvation, but also of typhus and other deadly diseases raging through the huts. *(Imperial War Museum, BU-4028)*

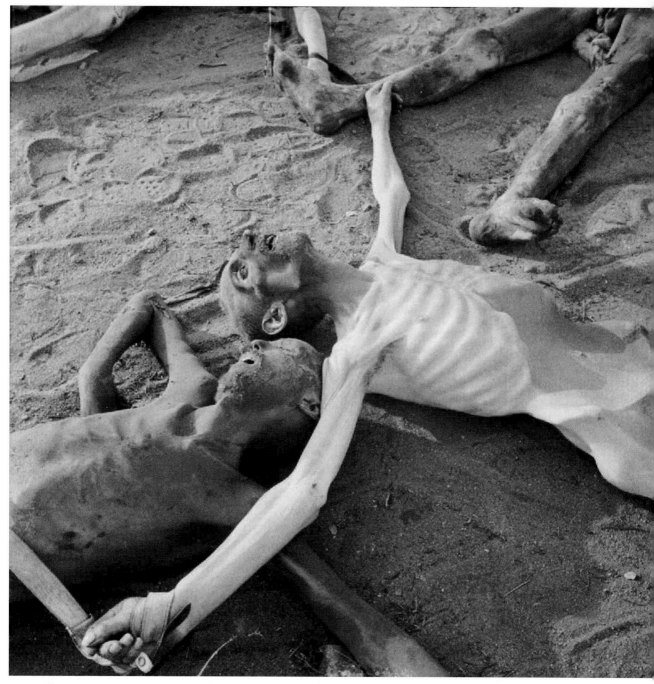

Two dead emaciated men soon to be buried in one of the mass graves inside the camp. Literally thousands of dead prisoners had to be buried as quickly as possible to reduce the epidemic of typhus which was threatening to kill the few survivors still barely clinging on to life. (*Imperial War Museum, BU-3760*)

The camp crematorium furnace used by the Germans to incinerate dead bodies. The Germans soon found that the furnace was useless in coping with the numbers dying daily in the camp. *(Imperial War Museum, BU-4004)*

Living quarters inside the wooden barracks of the camp. This photograph was taken after the liberation and a number of the wooden bunks have been broken up, possibly for fire wood. Living conditions inside these huts were horrific, but having a bunk was, by concentration camp standards, a luxury. (*National Archives*)

A British soldier watches on as inmates of the camp collect water and food. The advance units of the British Second Army that liberated Bergen-Belsen on 15 April were neither physically nor psychologically prepared for what they encountered when they arrived at the gates of the camp that day. British soldiers were numbed and nauseated by what they saw, smelled, and heard in the Luneburg forest. (*Imperial War Museum, BU-4022*)

The reality of Belsen and a true reminder of what these guards had inflicted on these hapless souls. Literally hundreds of dead naked bodies are sprawled out in a wooded area around the camp prior to burial in mass graves. (*Imperial War Museum, BU-4029*)

(*Opposite, top*) Living barracks 23. Female inmates perform the dreadful and degrading task of sorting the clothing of the dead. (*Imperial War Museum, BU-3722*)

(*Opposite, bottom*) More dead being moved by the inmates to special areas around the camp prior to mass burial. (*Imperial War Museum, BU-3724*)

A typical scene at Belsen. Two men lie dead on a mound of straw and earth, probably cleared out from one of the living quarters. Death had become a commonplace occurrence inside the camp. *(Imperial War Museum, BU-3732)*

Female prisoners trying to regain some dignity inside the camp and make use of the ground in front of the living barracks to cook. Two women can be seen cleaning their teeth, a luxury they probably had not had for some considerable time. *(National Archives)*

Female prisoners moving along the camp with their provisions in bags. By the appearance of these inmates they look relatively healthy, an indication that they are comparatively new to life at Belsen. *(National Archives)*

A photograph taken from one of the watchtowers showing the state of the camp. Clothing and dead bodies are strewn in heaps outside each building. Just prior to Belsen's liberation there had been a breakdown in the command structure of the camp. There were so many bodies to bury that disease from them caused many of the guards to desert, fearing they might catch typhus. *(Imperial War Museum, BU-4710)*

In front of a living barracks, bundles of clothing from the dead are strewn over the ground. Before the liberation of Belsen there was total disorder. Even a number of the SS personnel were out of control, killing and stealing whatever they could find from the dead. Corruption at Belsen, as with many other concentration camps across the Reich and Poland, had become widespread. (*Yad Vashem, 1377.12*)

An inmate scavenges amongst some ragged clothes found on the floor, more than likely from another dead prisoner. Around him are dead and half-starved survivors of the camp. During the last weeks of the camp's operation Kramer had been concerned that administration was breaking down. Camp life had deteriorated so much that many of the inmates simply did not have enough strength to get up. Many of the prisoners were badly emaciated, their arms and legs like matchsticks, their bones protruding through their skin. Many of those who had been evacuated to Belsen had been herded into the camp and left to die. Once they had died the corpses were left lying around. The stench of decomposition was overpowering. *(Imperial War Museum, BU-3766)*

Josef Kramer sits on a stool under the supervision of an armed British guard, who stares at his prisoner. (*Imperial War Museum, BU-3823*)

(*Opposite*) Two photographs showing a shackled Josef Kramer, commandant of Belsen, who has been arrested by British troops and escorted away under armed guard. Prior to the liberation of Belsen, the camp had descended into such disorganization that Kramer could no longer cope with the amount of new arrivals. He was particularly scathing towards his subordinates and as a result of the deteriorating situation encouraged his men to become even more vicious. The pressure was so enormous that often guards who had shown some degree of restraint towards the deportees were now observed whipping and beating women and children. Some murdered them with their own hands or shot dead anyone who would not respond quickly enough to an order. (*Imperial War Museum, BU-3822 and BU-3749*)

Another photograph of *SS-Hauptsturmführer* Josef Kramer taken just before the commencement of his trial. A British soldier stands armed behind the former Belsen commandant. *(Imperial War Museum, BU-9710)*

Kramer and Irma Grese are seen here together just before their trial. Kramer was reputed to be one of her many lovers and who had Grese permanently assigned to Belsen. To her female colleagues it seemed that *SS* overseer Grese wanted to remain at the typhus-ridden hell-hole just for the sake of her *SS* boyfriend. (*Imperial War Museum, BU-9745*)

Concentration camp guards rounded up following the liberation of the camp. (*Yad Vashem, 15C08*)

Arrested *SS Aufseherinnen*. Pictured are, Irene Haschke, Herta Bothe, Herta Ehlert, Johanna Bormann, Elisabeth Volkenrath, Getrud Sauer, Ilse Forster, Klara Opitz, Rosina Scheiber and Gertrud Neumann, among others. Block 317 is visible in the background. (*Yad Vashem, 18A09*)

Women concentration camp guards following their capture in the camp. It astounded British troops that these female guards were casually standing around chatting and smoking cigarettes waiting for their conquerors to arrive. All the women wore white brassards on their lower left tunic sleeves with a black cloth strip bearing the silver-threaded *SS Aufseherin* stamp, and either hobnailed jack boots or military issue dress shoes with black socks. One soldier recalled that many of the women had contorted, ugly facial expressions. *(Imperial War Museum, BU-4065)*

A photograph showing a mass grave. At that time as many as 500 a day were perishing from the long-term effects of starvation and disease. (*Imperial War Museum, BU-3778*)

(*Opposite, top*) A group of captured Belsen concentration camp guards have been rounded up by the British and are being given strict instructions on their daily duties. These duties would include clearing the dead with their bare hands and burying them in mass graves. (*Yad Vashem, 15B03*)

(*Opposite, bottom*) When the British arrived in Belsen they found around 10,000 unburied dead in addition to the mass graves already containing at least 40,000 more corpses. (*Imperial War Museum, BU-3741*)

Female concentration camp guards being forced by British troops to clear the dead with their bare hands and burying them in the mass graves. (*Imperial War Museum, BU-4032*)

SS troops bury the dead. (*Getty Images, United States Holocaust Memorial Museum courtesy of George Stein*)

A photograph showing the horrific scenes when some of the perpetrators of these terrible crimes against humanity were made to clear away the bodies of their victims. (*George Rodger [Time & Life Pictures]*)

(*Opposite*) The burials continued for days with both male and female guards being forced to undertake the clearing of the dead. (*George Rodger [Time & Life Pictures], Getty Images*)

Concentration camp guards being detailed on the clearing operation at Belsen. British troops were determined to make these men and women guards at least in some way accountable for their terrible actions. (*Imperial War Museum, BU-4023*)

British troops witnessing the appalling sight of concentration camp personnel under armed guard lifting the emaciated dead bodies of inmates onto a waiting open truck for burial. This vehicle would then take its cargo of corpses to a mass grave where other guards would be waiting to unload them. *(Imperial War Museum, BU-4024)*

A photograph showing women concentration camp guards lifting the dead from a truck and throwing the corpses into an undignified mass grave. *(Imperial War Museum, BU-4030)*

Concentration camp guards seen unloading the dead and taking them to the mass grave for burial. Armed British troops can be seen surrounding this work detail. (*Imperial War Museum, BU-4035*)

A bulldozer is being used by a British soldier to clear the dead and move these bodies into a mass grave. (*Imperial War Museum, BU-4058*)

SS guards, exhausted from their forced labour clearing the bodies of the dead, are allowed a brief rest by British soldiers, but are forced to take it by lying down in an empty grave face down. *(Imperial War Museum, BU-4094)*

Three photographs showing camp guards moving corpses to the mass burial site. (*Imperial War Museum, BU-4060, BU-4061 and BU-4191*)

SS troops after being ordered to bury their victims in mass graves are then forced to cover up the grave with sand and dirt. The British Army estimated there to be around 10,000 corpses lying strewn around Belsen camp. Former SS staff and Hungarian soldiers were used to dig the graves and bury the dead. On occasions a bulldozer was required to push the bodies into the graves due to the state of their decomposition. The British gave each grave an identity number which included the total number of bodies contained within. (*Imperial War Museum, BU-4273*)

Pictured here is Franz Hoessler, forced by the British to be photographed and filmed for British Movietone News, standing in front of a truck full of dead. Hoessler arrived at Belsen with his transport on 8 April 1945 and became deputy camp commander under Josef Kramer. It was not long before Hoessler began shooting and beating the prisoners. On 15 April 1945, when the British liberated the camp, Hoessler was found hiding among the prisoners in camouflaged clothing and was detained with the remaining SS staff by a unit of the British Army. *(Yad Vashem)*

The first of five photographs showing both male and female guards loading the dead onto trucks, destined for the huge burial pits that have been specially dug. A large number of prisoners died after the liberation. Of the 40,000 surviving prisoners found by the Allies in the camp on 15 April 1945, some 14,000 were to die by the end of June. The British were completely overwhelmed by the death rate. *(Yad Vashem)*

(Opposite) Two photographs showing guards being forced under armed British supervision to remove dead bodies. The mass graves that were dug to bury these poor dead souls could hold up to 5,000 corpses. The guards were deliberately made to use their bare hands to bury the dead, many of whom were ravaged with contagious diseases. *(Yad Vashem)*

Female guards placing the dead into one of the large mass graves. The female *Aufseherinnen* were more arrogant and sadistic than their male guard counterparts. The British soldiers were fully aware of this, and immediately arrested them and put them to work. (*Yad Vashem*)

In a frame from the film *The True Glory*, photographer Sergeant Mike Lewis from the British Film and Photographic Unit is caught on camera as he films the removal and burial of diseased and starved-to-death inmates following the liberation of the camp. (*Imperial War Museum, FLM-1232*)

A half-full truck of dead prisoners from Belsen destined for their mass burial by captured German guards.
(*National Archives*)

Appendix I

Belsen Concentration Camp Staff

Name	Camp Position
Hauptsturmführer Benno Martin Adolph	Doctor
Jacques Albala	Jüdenältester Sternlager
Unterscharführer Bruno Hugo Albrecht	
Aldona	Blockältester Block 201
Colonel Jenö Alterjay	Hungarìan Guard Company
Hauptsharführer Arthur Kurt Andrae	
Hermann Andriesse	Deputy Lagerältester Star Camp
Hauptmann Arenkens	Stellv. Bataillonskommandeur
Ruth Astrosini / Astrosene	Phone Operator
Kapo August	Chief Kapo Camp 2
Aufseherin Ault / Alt / Olt	
Antoni Aurdzieg	Blockältester Block 12
Heinz Bad	
Colonel Zoltan Balo	Hungarian Guard Company
Hauptscharführer Ernst Balz	Deputy Lagerführer
Unterscharführer Erich Barsch	Medical Orderly Camp 2
Rottenführer Bartel	Wood Kommando
Adam Bartschiniski / Berschinski	Stubendienst Block 12 / Deputy Blockältester
Arnost Basch	Functionary
Aufseherin Beda / Bade	
Kapo Bellenech	
Oberscharführer Bentwick	i/c MB87 Bergen-Belsen Barracks
Kapo Berling	
Aufseherin Beseke / Besoke	Kitchen D(3) East
Rottenführer Johann Besemer	Medical Orderly Camp 2
Leutnant Deszö Bibo	Hungarian Guard Company
Bernhard Blank	
Eric Boerfler / Börfler	Prisoner Medic
Aufseherin Johanna / Juana Bormann	Looked after the pigs behind Block 9
Aufseherin Herta Bothe / Lange	

Friedrich / Fritz Branders	Kommandoführer
Joseph Braunitzer	Hungarian Guard Company
Hauptsturmführer Otto Brenneis	
SS Mann Peter Brüfach	
Herbert Buhr	
Oberscharführer Siegfried Buhr	
Medislaw Burgraf	Blockältester / Stubendienst Block 19
Sturmmann Helmut Busse	
Oberscharführer Hermann Büttner	Medic
Wladyslaw Byrski	Block Orderly Block 15
Oberscharführer Otto Calesson / Kulessa	
Obersturmführer Hermann Campe	Schutzhaftlagerführer
Kapo Kasimir / Kazimierz Alexander Cegielski / Rydzewski	
Rottenführer Charon	
Josef Chudý	
Hauptmann Cramm	Intelligence
Kapo Sternlager Kasimir Czubiński / Czubialski	
Unterscharführer Hermann Deidok	
Walter Donning	
Rottenführer Wilhelm Dörr	
F Dunkelmann	
Unterscharführer Karl Egersdorf / Egersdörfer	Food Storeman
Aufseherin Herta Ehlert / Naumann / Ließ	
Unterscharführer Wilhelm Emman	
Oberscharführer Wilhelm Emmerich	Rapportführer
Aufseherin Gertrude Feist / Fiest	
Rottenführer Helmut Fink	Electrician
Sturmbannführer Johann Hermann Fischer	Lagerarzt
Aufseherin Lisbeth / Liesbeta Fitzner / Fritzner	
Rottenführer Karl Flrazich / Francioh / Franzioh / Firazisch / Franzisch	Commander Kitchen D(3) East
Sergeant Joszef Forgach	Hungarian Guard Company
Aufseherin Ida Förster	Kitchen D(3) West
Aufseherin Ilse Förster	Kitchen B(1)
Obersturmführer Fox	
Frieda Frankel / Franka / Franken	Blockältester Block 199
Untersturmführer Wilhelm / Wilheim Frerichs	Officer Commanding Criminal Department
Unterscharführer Karl Freudenberger	
Obersturmführer Friedrich	Political Department
Aufseherin Friedrich / Friedrichs	Vegetable Kommando
Unterscharführer Josef Friedsam	Blockführer
Paul Fritsch	
Paul Fritzner	

Frühlingsdorf	
Hauptscharführer Fuchs	
Halina Furstenberg	Stubendienst
Leutnant Gabor Gambos	Hungarian Guard Company
Unterscharführer Franz Gatschengis	
Unterscharführer Freidrich / Fritz Gaus	Schuhkommandoführer
Unterscharführer Hermann Gauseweg	
Scharführer Geissler	In charge of Kitchen No. 4
Unterscharführer Wilhelm Genth	Medic
Unterscharführer Gerhard Gläser	
Albert Goedeke	Administration / Clothing
Aufseherin Nelly Goldstein	
Aufseherin Hildegard Gollasch	Rapportführerin
Generalmajor Friedrich Gombart	Commandant
Alois / Aloys Götzy	Driver
Rottenführer Alfred Grams	
Oberaufseherin Irma Ilse Ida Grese	Arbeitsdienstführerin and Rapportführerin
Unterscharführer Josef Groß	
Oberst Erhard Grosan	Commander Tank Training School Bergen-Belsen Barracks
Rottenführer Ferdinand Grosse (Unconfirmed)	
Dr Grossfeld	Lagerältester
Rottenführer Ladislaw Gura	Guard
Estera Guterman	Stubendienst
Stubenältester Güterman	
Adolf Gutermann	
Hauptsturmführer Adolf Haas	Kommandant
Aufseherin Hildegard Hahnel / Hehnal / Halmel	
Eugen Hahnert	
Unterscharführer Josef Hamer / Hammer	Blockführer
Kapo Sternlager Haneke	
Walter Hanke	Lagerältester Häftlingslager
Oberscharführer Hanzig	
Franz Harich / Horich	Guard?
Oberst Karl Harries	Commander Bergen-Belsen barracks
Oberscharführer Hartwig	
Aufseherin Irene Haschke	Kitchen D(3) East
Oberscharführer Franz Wolfgang Hatzinger	
Häusler / Hausler	
Rottenführer Heinz Lüder Heidemann	Blockführer
Hans Heinrich	
Oberscharführer Heinz	
Scharführer Heinz	
Oberaufseherin Gertrud Elli Heise / Heize / Senff	

Oberscharführer Hermann Helbig	
Oberscharführer Oskar Georg Helbig	
Aufseherin Anna Hempel / Herdlitschke	Kitchen A(2)
Sturmmann Stefan Hermann	Guard
Scharführer Friedrich Herzog / Hertzoch / Hertzog	
Oberscharführer Theodore Heuskel / Heskel	Commander Kitchen A(2)
Kapo Hilde	
Oberscharführer Heinrich Hilmer	Administration / Toolstoreman
Kapo Phillip Himmel	
Christian Höckling	Kitchen führer Sternlager
Leutnant Hohmann	Adjutant
Hauptscharführer Jan Holst	
Heinrich Hoppenstedt	
Horra	Military Secretary
Hauptsturmführer Rudolf (Dr) Horstmann	Medical Officer
Obersturmführer Franz Hössler / Hoessler / Hessler	Kommandant Camp No. 2
Unterscharführer Karl Heinrich Hykes	
Otto (Dr) Imgart	
Ingra	Lagerältester
Aufseherin Jabasch / Jabusch	
Hauptscharführer Franz Jäckel	
Obersturmführer Wilhelm / Willi (Dr) Jäger	Medical Officer Häftlingslager
Schütze Rudolf Jankowski	Wachcompanie (Camp Guard)
Scharführer Nikolaus Jänner / Jenner / Jonner	Commander Kitchen D(3) West
Karl Joachim	
Rottenführer Johanns	Political Department
Isaak Judalewsky / Judelewsky	Blockältester Block No 2
Ladislaw Judkovitz	Functionary
Stanislaus / Stanislaw Kacyska / Kaoyska / Kaczyska / Kaeyska	Blockältester
Rottenführer G Kahsmann	Political Department
Hauptscharführer Josef Kaiser	
Aufseherin Hildegard Kambach / Kanbach	
Sturmmann Johann Kasanicky / Kasainitzky / Kasainiky	Blockführer
Kapo Kasimir Kasinski	
Untersturmführer Eric / Erich (Dr) Kather	
Katia	Lagerältester Small Women's Camp.
Harry Kaufmann	
Aufseherin Magdalene Kessel	
Kapo T. Wally Kierschke	
Eva Kilemann	Blockältester Block 205
Anton / Auson Kinkartz / Kinkraz	
Sergeant Ferenc Kiss	Hungarian Guard Company
Hauptscharführer Kitz	
Rottenführer Klahr	

Hauptsturmführer Friedrich / Fritz Klein	Medical Officer
Aufseherin Charlotte Klein / Hoffmann	
Emil Klese / Klesse	
Wika Klimczewska	Deputy Blockältester Block 26
Untersturmführer Kurt Klipp	Lagerführer / Kramer's 2 i/c
Sturmmann Josef Klippel	
Rottenführer Emil Kltscho / Klische / Klischo / Klichow / Kleso	
Aufseherin Gisela / Gisella / Giselle Koblischek	Kitchen No A(2) or Gemusekeller
Aufseherin Johanna Koch	Kitchen Commander
Aufseherin Anneliese Kohlmann	
Stefan Konrad	
Helene Koper / Kopper / Korperova	Blockälteste Block 27 / 205 / 224
(Dr) Korska	Doctor Camp 2
Kapo Edgar Elias Kounio / Cugnio	Arbeitsführer
Aufseherin Binia Kowarz	
Unterscharführer Georg Kraft	Lagerführer and Cook
Schütze Franz Krahl	
Oberscharführer Krakauer	
Hauptsturmführer Josef Kramer	Kommandant
Hauptscharführer Paul Kreutzer	
Sturmbannführer Richard (Dr) Krieger	Lagerarzt
Unterscharführer Friedrich / Fritz Kroh	Häftlinger Canteen
Aufseherin Ingeborg Krüger	
Unterscharführer Kuckertz	Office Clerk
Hauptscharführer Josef Kuhn	Administration
Unterscharführer Heinz Kühnemann	
Unterscharführer Walter Kümmel	
Aufseherin Joanna Kurd	
Robert Kurt / Kurz	SS Doctor
Oberstandartenjunker Alfred (Dr) Kurzke	Lagerarzt
Obersturmführer Friedrich Küster	Administration
Unterscharführer Lademacher	Administration
Sturmmann Lamac / Lamac	
Schütze Ferdinand Lange	Wachcompanie (Camp Guard)
Aufseherin Lehmann	Vegetable Kommando
Schütze Richard Lehmann	Wachcompanie (Camp Guard)
Unterscharführer Ludwig Lenz	
Aufseherin Martha Anna Linke	
Untersturmführer Walter Josef Linsmeier / Linsmeyer	Dentist
Rottenführer Adolf Linz	
Kapo Hilde Lippman	Kitchen I
Aufseherin Hildegard Lippmann	
Aufseherin Elli Lippmann / Springer	
Aufseherin Hilde Lisiewitz	Vegetable Kommando

Arbeitsdienst Hildegard Löbauer / Lohbauer	
Aufseherin Marta Löbelt	Telephonist
Kapo Hilda Löffer / Löffler	
Kapo Ilse Lothe	Vegetable Kommando
Oberscharführer Elimar / Helmer Lübbe / Lübben	Rapportführer
Oberst Kurt Lucius	
Paul Maas	
Unterscharführer Mabel	
Antoni Maer	Blockälteste
Josef Magiera	
Hans Mais / May	
Peter Leonard (Dr) Makar	Internee Doctor
Aufseherin Malchartzeck	
Mangel	Nightguard Block 12
Anton Marsch	
Unterscharführer Friedrich / Fritz Mathes	
Maximillian	
Unterscharführer Wilhelm May	Commander SS Kitchen
Oberscharführer Walter Melcher	Entlausung
Hauptsturmführer Ernst Julius Kurt / Curt Max Meyer	Commander Guard Company
Larion (Dr) Michailowski	Doctor
Kapo Stanislaw Migala	
Ernst Mittag	Revierschreiber Häftlingslager
W Moog	
Hauptsturmführer Ernst Mös / Moes	RSHA
Unterscharführer Arthur Müller	Blockführer / Drains and Sewers
Scharführer Friedrich / Fritz Müller	Food Storeman
Unterscharführer Hermann Müller	Blockführer
Unterscharführer Hermann Werner Müller	Food Storeman
E Nebe	
Katherine Neiger	Lagerälteste / Clerk
Major Otto Neue	
Aufseherin Gertrud Neumann	
Oberscharführer Oberhaid	
Feliks Oksay	Hungarian Guard Company
Aufseherin Klara Opitz	In the kitchen of Block 9 and in charge of some female working parties.
Aufseherin Orlt	Kitchen D(3)
Kapo Vladislav / Wladyslaw Ostrowoski / Ostroski	Block 19
Unterscharführer Wilhelm August Otte	Deputy Rapportführer / Blockführer / Clerk
Oberscharführer Walter Otto	Supervisor of the electricians
Kapo Stefan Patai	
Leutnant Laszlo Pato	Hungarian Guard Company
Unterscharführer Albert Petry	Clothing

Karl Petzoldt	
Berta Pezimma	
Ansgar / Anchor Pichen / Pinchen	Commander Kitchen B(1)
Aldona Pietrkiewicz	Blockälteste Block 201
Pinner	Blockältester Sternlager
Aufseherin Charlotte Pliquet	
Sturmmann Pohl	Commander Kitchen D(3) and 2 i/c Kitchen No. 4
Antoni Polanski	Medical Assistant after liberation
Jan Polit	
Unterscharführer Wilhelm Pott	Political Department
Oberscharführer Joachim Pyrskala	
Oberscharführer Walter Friedrich Wilhelm Quakernack	
Scharführer Josef Ramer	
Unterscharführer Rang	Acting Adjutant
Oberscharführer Kurt Raschack	
Unterscharführer Friedrich / Fritz Rau	Arbeitsdienstführer / Kommandoführer
Oberscharführer Karl Heinrich / Heinz Reddehase	Schuhkommandoführer / Commander Aussenlager Hambühren
Rottenführer Heinrich Reents	
Hauptscharführer Johann Reinhart	Clothing
Aufseherin Gertrud(e) Reinhold / Rheinholt / Brätigam	
Rottenführer Friedrich Wilhelm Rex	
Richter	Medical Orderly
Aufseherin Ronne	Kitchen D(3)
Rottenführer Rosegger	
Johann Rosemar	
Aufseherin Erna Rosenthal	Kitchen A(2)
Johanne Roth	Stubenälteste Block 199
Karl Rothe	Prisoner Nurse
Sarna	Nightguard Block 12
Aufseherin Gertrud(e) Sauer	
Obersturmführer Hans Schaaf	Administration
Rottenführer Anton Schacht	Guard
Oberstleutnant Scharwächter	
Aufseherin Rosina / Rosira Scheiber	
Hauptsturmführer Hugo Schlegel	
Ignatz Schlomowicz / Schlomowitz / Schlomoivicz	Blockältester
Kapo Oscar Schmedidzt / Schmitz	Lagerältester Camp 2
Hauptsturmführer Ernst Heinrich (Dr) Schmidt	Medical Officer Camp 2
Oberst Hanns Schmidt	Bergen – Belsen Barracks
Aufseherin Johanne Schmidt	Night Guard Block 199
Elsa Schmidt / Schmitt	
Oberscharführer Karl Schmidt / Schmitt	

Sturmbannführer Alfred (Dr) Schnabel	Medical Officer / Lagerarzt
Aufseherin Emmi Schotig	
Oberscharführer Heinrich / Hansi Schreirer / Schreier / Schrierer	Blockführer / Political Department
Sturmscharführer Friedrich / Fritz Schultes	Political Department
Unterscharführer Walter Schwank	Sanitätsdienstgrad
SS Mann Josef Schwarzhuber	
Hauptscharführer Franz Seemann	
Obersturmführer Siegfried (Dr) Seidl	Commander Political Department
Kurt Sendsitzsky / Senxsitzky	
Sofia Seyfarth	
Josephine Singer	Blockälteste Block 198
Slottke (Not confirmed)	
Eliasz Sołowiejczyk	Lagerälteste
Hermann Sommer	Prisoner Doctor / Medic
Sturmmann Stefan Sommer	Wachcompanie (Camp Guard)
Civilian Wilhelm Spahr	Police
Civilian Erich Speelman / Spielmann	Criminal Secretary Political Department (Gestapo)
Aufseherin Ursula Sporn	
Stanisława / Stefania Staroska / Starostka / Starostki	Lagerälteste Großes Frauenlager
Sturmmann Konrad Stefan	
Otto Steffensenn	
Aufseherin Ilse Steinbusch / Steinbruch	
Hauptscharführer Paul Steinmetz	Technician / Electrician
Stern	Administration
Stibitz	Rapportführer
Unterscharführer Heinz Stöcker	Blockführer
Hauptscharführer Franz Xaver Stöfel / Starfl / Stärfel	Lagerleiter
Eva / Ewa Krystyka Stojowska	Blockälteste Block 201
Oberscharführer Arthur Stolle	
Mevrouw Nettie Stoppelmann	Blockälteste
Obersturmführer Gustav Strese / Stresse / Streese	Lagerführer
Unterscharführer Heinrich Strohecker	Mail / Post Censor
Stuber	Blockführer
Kapo Lidia Sunschein	Kitchen A(2)
Roman Svistl	Watchtower Guard
Paula Synger	Clerk Block 224
Untersturmführer Heinz / Henig Tacke	Guard Company
Marian Tatarczuk	
Wilhelm Tell	
Willi / Wily / Willy Thermann / Thorman / Thormann	
Schütze Tibor Toth	Wachcompanie (Camp Guard)
Traur	
Hauptscharführer Franz-Xaver Trenkle	Schutzhäftlagerführer

Unterscharführer Triebel	
Uhlmann / Ullmann	Medical Orderly Camp No. 2
Leutnant Geza Ujvary	Hungarian Guard Company
Unidentified	
Cadet Officer Karoly Vajna	Hungarian Guard Company
Kapo Michael Vassiliew / Vassiliev	
Hauptsturmführer Wilhelm Vogler	Administration / Food Supply
Oberaufseherin Elisabeth Volkenrath / Mühlan	
Major Ernst von Briesen	Bataillonskommandeur
Hauptmann von der Ohe	Geschäftz.
Paweł Włodawski	Lagerältester
Oberscharführer Theodor Wagner	
Aufseherin Frieda Walter	Kitchen D(3) West / Kiesel Kommando
O Warnecke / Wernicke	
Oberscharführer Ernst Weber	Kommandant's Teleprinter Operator
Hauptscharführer Peter Weingartner	Blockführer
Zdenek (Dr) Weisner	Doctor
Josef Weiss	Judenältester Sternlager
Schütze Josef Wenzel	Kitchen No. 1
Rottenführer Heinrich Wernecke / Wernicke	
Unterscharführer Heinrich Werner	
Sturmmann Wessel	Kitchen No. A(2)
Rottenführer Wessely / Wesseli	Kitchen No. 1
Oberleutnant Wigger	Offz. Z.b.V.
Elisabeth Will	
Unterscharführer Friedrich Wille	Administration
Unterscharführer Michael Willkomm	Standesbeamten Political Department
Wilmschen	Foodstore in Bergen-Belsen barracks
Unterscharführer Arnold Wilmschen	Political Department
Eduard / Edvard Wirths / Wirtz	Doctor
Unterscharführer Joachim Wolf	
Unterscharführer Adolf Wünschen	
Helena Zachaczewski	Blockälteste Block 26
Bruno Zamoray	Hungarian Guard Company
Wenzel Zankl	
Aufseherin Susanne Zielonka	
Aufseherin Erna Zietelmann / Hentschel	
Kapo Erich Zoddel	Blockälteste / Lagerälteste

Appendix II

Sentences given to Staff

Name	Sentence
Josef Kramer	Death, executed on December 13, 1945
Fritz Klein	Death, executed on December 13, 1945
Peter Weingärtner	Death, executed on December 13, 1945
Franz Hössler	Death, executed on December 13, 1945
Karl Franzioh	Death, executed on December 13, 1945
Ansgar Pichen	Death, executed on December 13, 1945
Franz Stofel (or Stärfl)	Death, executed on December 13, 1945
Wilhelm Dörr	Death, executed on December 13, 1945
Irma Grese	Death, executed on December 13, 1945
Elisabeth Volkenrath	Death, executed on December 13, 1945
Johanna Bormann	Death, executed on December 13, 1945
Otto Kulessa	15 years, released May 7, 1955
Heinrich Schreirer	15 years, released September 3, 1950
Hertha Ehlert	15 years, released May 7, 1953
Ilse Förster	10 years, released December 21, 1951
Hertha Bothe	10 years, released December 21, 1951
Irene Haschke	10 years, released December 21, 1951
Gertrud Sauer	10 years, released December 21, 1951
Anna Hempel	10 years, released April 21, 1951
Gertrud Feist	5 years, released August 11, 1949
Frieda Walter	3 years, released November 16, 1948
Hilde Lisiewicz	1 year, released November 16, 1946
Georg Krafft	Acquitted
Josef Klippel	Acquitted
Fritz Mathes	Acquitted
Karl Egersdörfer	Acquitted
Walter Otto	Acquitted
Erich Barsch	Acquitted
Ida Förster	Acquitted
Klara Opitz	Acquitted
Charlotte Klein	Acquitted
Hildegard Hähnel	Acquitted

Notes

Notes

Notes

Notes

Notes

Notes

Notes